INTERNATIONAL ONLINE TEACHING

HOW HIGH-SCHOOL TEACHERS CAN EARN FULL-TIME INCOME BY TEACHING JUST FOUR HOURS A WEEK

NERVANA ELKHADRAGY, PHARM.D., PH.D.

CONTENTS

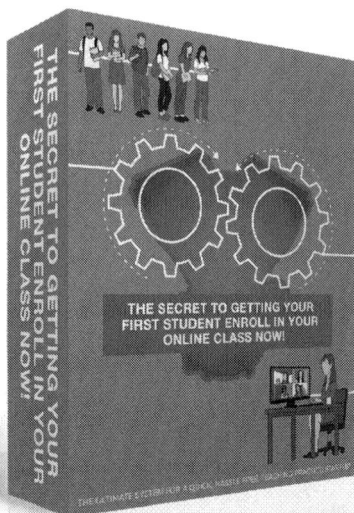

A Special Gift for Teachers
Are you interested in independent teaching? Included with your purchase is our FREE guide: *"The Secret to Getting Your First Student Enroll in Your Online Class Now! The Ultimate System for a Quick, Hassle free, Teaching Practice Startup."*

Visit the link below and let us know which email address to deliver it to.

https://www.teachinternationally.online/3secrets

INTRODUCTION

Imagine a society where students as young as Grade 10 are under such immense pressure to achieve A+ results in almost all subjects that they seek tutorship in every single subject. Their parents scour the internet looking for independent English-speaking teachers skilled at helping learners achieve top marks through online tutoring. The pressure is on; if these students don't achieve top grades they won't be accepted to study for a degree at an "elite" university. Without a degree, they will be seen as failures because, in this society, a degree means everything.

This society exists. Tens of thousands of 9th to 12th Grade learners in many countries are actively looking for English-speaking teachers in various subjects: from math to sciences to English, and everything in between.

What's more, they aren't looking for teachers in their hometown—they are looking for online teachers who are proficient in teaching their curriculum in English, regardless of location.

That online teacher could be you.

I am Dr. Nervana Elkhadragy. I currently teach more than one hundred students from nine different countries, and it takes up only four hours of my time per week. Thanks to my online practice, I earn enough additional income that I am no longer drowning in student loans. I don't have to leave the job I love, and I don't have to pursue a different career for an extra income. I use my skills and my experience as a teacher, embrace the advantages that technology has brought us, and teach international students via platforms such as Zoom.

In this book, I aim to share with you how I started my teaching practice. I will guide you through the entire process, using examples from my personal experience. I learned by doing and now I'm going to show you how to do it too. You don't have to experience any unnecessary pain—just follow my advice. By the end of this book, you will fully understand how to attract students to your online program without having to spend money on marketing. I will also show you how to help your students achieve the best results. And all of this without having to quit your day job.

My mission is to take your teaching career and transform it to the next level.

During the 1990s, Steve Ells—founder of Chipotle—realized he needed to relocate his Mexican fast-food idea out of the already taco-flooded San Francisco. He knew people loved Mexican food and he knew he made delicious tacos, but he needed to make his tacos available in an area with greater demand. Fast-forward thirty years, Chipotle is a multimillion-dollar franchise with more than 45,000 employees in over 2,000 locations in five countries.[1] The success of Ells' franchise could probably be traced back to a single decision: Take a product that's popular in one location and introduce it to a different location where there is a need for it.

You are Steve Ells. Your teaching skills are the Mexican food. Students in other countries in need of academic help are the taco-hungry regions, waiting eagerly to buy your tacos.

Any teacher can make a success of tutoring—teaching—internationally online, no matter what subject you teach or how many years of teaching experience you have.

You may have considered starting a new business to supplement your salary and there are myriad considerations that can make it seem incredibly daunting. It requires you to learn new skills such as marketing, driving traffic to your business, and optimizing advertisements. What's more, most business ideas require a lot of money as an initial investment and a lot of time before they see any profit.

If you decided to open a business that involved the buying and selling of goods, you would have to purchase inventory, which could cost thousands of dollars. You would then need somewhere to sell your products from—either a physical or online store—and market your products. It may take time for the products to sell. While you wait, you would have to pay rent if the store is physical. If it's an online store, you will have the expense of setting up the e-commerce site and search engine optimization (SEO) so that people can find your products online. Not only is this time-consuming, but it can also be incredibly expensive!

What if I told you that you could start a business with little capital outlay? All that is required are the skills you already have, i.e., teaching. The business I am referring to is an international tutoring practice. Although the term "tutoring" technically means teaching a small group, throughout this book I will show you that this small group can quickly grow into a large number of students and so I will use "tutoring" and "teaching" interchangeably. You are likely to start with small groups, but it won't take long for you to grow your practice and become an online "teacher" of a large number of students.

We've already established that there is a need for this kind of service. In many parts of the world, students are taught English curricula even though their first language is not English. Parents are willing to pay English-speaking teachers from English-speaking countries like the United States (US) to tutor them, so they excel at school. And, due to the COVID-19 pandemic, you already know how to teach online.

Thankfully, despite all the advancements in technology, teachers are unlikely to ever be replaced by robots, nor will teaching become automated. There is nothing that can replace the interaction between teacher and students. Teachers will always be needed by students and appreciated by parents.

If you're a teacher and you're living paycheck-to-paycheck, I have great news for you! You are needed. There is a considerable demand for your teaching skills.

This book is a comprehensive guide on how to use the skills you have for the job you love, to earn excellent additional income. Plus, you don't need *any* business skills, nor do you need a massive monetary investment. You just need to do one thing: **teach**.

Isn't that amazing? Do what you love and earn huge amounts of extra income for doing it. I had always thought that teaching doesn't pay, and I accepted this limiting belief. So, I elected to be a struggling educator. I chose to be a life-long learner and spread my knowledge. However, that came with a price—enormous student loans and a rather limited salary. As a result, I ended up borrowing lots and lots of money just to survive.

Overall, I had accumulated a six-figure debt because I followed my dreams. This debt required a monthly payment of $3,500, which is more than half of my monthly paycheck and I thought, "This isn't fair."

I started asking questions.

Why should I live a suboptimal life financially just so I can do the job I love?

Why should I be in so much debt despite my strong skillset and multiple degrees?

Why do I have to choose between money and profession?

And that's what I want all teachers to know—it doesn't have to be that way.

You can still do what you love—teaching—while earning a decent amount of money that doesn't force you to borrow just to survive.

I'm not here to talk about the broken system and the low pay; I'm here to help you. If you're like me and you *love* teaching, but you'd also love to live a lifestyle that doesn't put you in debt, then you're in the right place. In this book, I'll show you exactly how to do that.

I wanted to increase my income without investing any money and I wanted to do something that would work right away. If you want similar results, then keep reading.

The idea that I will be presenting to you in this book is an untapped opportunity that very few people are taking advantage of. No other book explains this model or goes into such detail about the nitty-gritty of getting an international tutoring practice off the ground—in that, this book is unique.

I have first-hand experience in everything I am telling you, and I'm sharing my real-life experiences with you.

If at first some of the words or terms don't make sense, don't worry because everything will be explained in detail throughout the book. When you're done, if you want more, I will provide you with a link where you can obtain additional training.

In this book, we will cover the following topics:

Chapter 1: Discover the Opportunity

Online teaching allows you to reach students everywhere. There is a great demand for teachers and tutors: your skills are the solution to a global problem. It requires a long-term commitment, but the demand equals opportunity, so you can *expect* success.

Chapter 2: Getting Started

The first step to success is getting started. This chapter will introduce you to the curriculum, including why it is popular with international students. We will also take a detailed look at the exam boards, the subjects they offer, and how grading and assessments work.

Chapter 3: Preparing Students for Exams

This chapter is divided into two parts. Part 1 details the value of past exam papers, which are free and available online. They will add value to your student's learning experience and can be used as a resource in your teaching practice.

Part 2 will detail the value of enrolling in a marking workshop, which will equip you to help your students attain their best possible exam outcomes. I will walk you through the process with a step-by-step guide.

Chapter 4: Establishing Yourself as an Expert

Chapter 4 is divided into two parts. Part 1 will explain why you should engage with people on social media and includes details on the "need" to build an audience, what platforms to focus on, and how the various platforms work.

Part 2 starts by explaining the ins and outs of providing free value on social media and in your groups. Then, I provide tips on managing your own groups and hosting a successful live session to draw potential students to your course.

Chapter 5: Communicating with Parents and Accepting Payments

Chapter 5 is divided into two parts. Part 1 is full of experiential advice about dealing with parents. I will give you a list of questions you can expect parents to ask and some questions for you to ask them in return. I will help you prepare for calls with parents, including overcoming any negative issues with the right attitude and persuading parents that you are the right teacher for their child.

Part 2 contains practical advice about how best to handle your administrative work, and we'll look at a few platforms that you could use for receiving international funds.

Chapter 6: When Would You Need a Website?

In this chapter, we explore when and why you will need a website for your teaching practice. Though a website is not essential, it's nice to have. It's not only for online exposure—it's for showcasing your resources in an organized and professional way.

You don't need a website developer to build your website. There are several platforms you can choose between to make your own. They are all user-friendly and will produce a professional-looking site, to make your life easier. We'll also look at what pages you need and what resources you can add to your website.

Chapter 7: Secrets to Scaling Your Practice

When you do your job well, your students will get good grades. Your teaching practice will grow through word-of-mouth, advertising, and other resources that I will share with you. You only have twenty-four hours in a day, so you will have to adopt time multipliers (aka, time savers) when your practice grows. Being well organized and outsourcing some of your responsibilities are two things you will need to do to enable your practice to reach its full potential.

> *"The amount of money we receive will always be in a direct ratio to the demand for what we do, our ability to do it, and the difficulty in replacing us."*
>
> — *EARL NIGHTINGALE*

Teachers are irreplaceable and much needed, yet they don't earn the same as others with comparable degrees. Teachers' salary deficit has been growing steadily for decades. You may think that our real-life situations disprove the validity of Earl Nightingale's quote. I'll admit, there was a time I believed so. Then, I discovered a way to use my gift as an educator to meet a huge demand and, in doing so, my earning potential grew exponentially.

When I started my online teaching practice I had two students. Within a few months, another three joined. The following year, I had twenty-five students enroll for my online teaching sessions, and now I teach more than one hundred students. How did I achieve such astronomical growth in just two academic years? That is precisely what I plan to show you throughout this book. By the time you reach the end, you will be equipped to establish a successful international teaching practice for yourself.

Scan the QR code to watch this short training video called: How to earn $1200 per hour.

DISCOVER THE OPPORTUNITY

"Once your mindset changes, everything on the outside will change along with it."

— *STEVE MARABOLI*

R ecognizing the big opportunity is half the battle. Having a fixed mindset or adopting limiting beliefs about this opportunity will hold you back. As a teacher, I am sure you are aware of the power of the mind. You probably have first-hand experience of students who had "made up their minds" that they would never be able to do math or chemistry and, as a result, they probably never will.

Countless quotes have been written about how the right mindset can help you attain success. I could list a whole string of them here. Hundreds of books have been written about mindset and people dedicate their lives to becoming mindset coaches. Why? Because the battle is won or lost in the mind. Once you've decided to succeed, very little can stand in your way. On the flip side, unless you make up your mind to succeed—or even worse, if you believe you *can't* succeed—your chances of success are slim to none.

So, although the objective of this book is to teach you how to become a successful, international online teacher, I'd be wasting your time if I didn't address the importance of having a winner's mindset right at the beginning of this exciting endeavor.

RECOGNIZING THE GAP

I teach more than one hundred students from nine different countries. Considering that over 600 million students enrolled for high school worldwide in 2019,[1] I would say teachers are profoundly needed in every subject.

Statistics aside, I teach Ordinary Level Chemistry only. However, I have had a parent call and ask me to *please* teach their child in Advanced Level. When I said I couldn't, she begged me. Her words were, "There are very few teachers tutoring Advanced Level—there's a huge gap here!"

Aside from the fact that I'm only teaching one hundred out of thousands of Ordinary Level students, there are still all the Advanced Level students also looking for teachers. And that's just chemistry. What about math, science, English, and all the other subjects? Students who need to get straight-A results are looking for a tutor in *every* subject.

Online teaching allows you to reach students *everywhere*

You will probably not be tutoring students who live in the US. There are many countries where students are taught in English, even when it is not their native language. These students seek English-speaking teachers, which is advantageous to teachers like you and me.

My students hail from countries such as Egypt, Saudi Arabia, the United Arab Emirates, Kuwait, Qatar, Oman, Turkey, Tunisia, and Singapore. There is no need for you to be intimidated by teaching students overseas. They are highly educated, smart, well-mannered, and all too grateful for your help. They all speak English fluently. Some parents may not speak English very well, but they will understand; therefore, you don't have to worry about language barriers. Students in the Middle East learn all subjects in English, using the American or British curriculum.

Yousef, an Egyptian Grade 10 student under my tutorship wants to be a pediatrician. University tuition in Egypt is government-funded and, therefore, free. That should be great news for Yousef and other students like him. Except there is a catch. To be accepted to the university, Yousef has to get A+ grades in all eight of his O-Level subjects and an A+ in two of his A-Level subjects. Yousef is under huge pressure. He needs a teacher to help him with each subject outside of his high school classes, and because he is following an English curriculum, his parents have sought English-speaking tutors, regardless of their locations.

Modern technology has made it possible for people to communicate across oceans. The COVID-19 pandemic forced teachers and students to learn how to work online. Rather than kicking against technology and letting the new teaching methods become a stumbling block, we can embrace the changes and the opportunities they bring.

There is much demand for teachers and tutors

Teaching is a calling. Why else would dedicated teachers work for less remuneration than other college graduates in comparable positions? Teachers leave the profession for various reasons; however, the three most common are low pay, challenging classroom conditions, and lack of training. The Economic Policy Institute (EPI) estimates that there is a shortage of 110,000 teachers in the US,[2] and this is a worldwide trend.

Unfortunately, this means that students are often not getting the attentive teaching they need to achieve the A+ results they so desperately want. So, they seek extra tuition—and that's where educators who are passionate about teaching and who are willing to step outside the traditional classroom can make a difference.

Find a solution for every problem

"What is the difference between an obstacle and an opportunity? Our attitude toward it. Every opportunity has a difficulty, and every difficulty has an opportunity."

— J. SIDLOW BAXTER

The world is full of people who see problems everywhere and quit if they encounter a stumbling block. You don't want to be one of them.

Some of the reasons and excuses teachers give for not wanting to try new things, and stumbling blocks that cause them to quit, are:

"I already teach full-time."

"I'm still new to teaching."

"Technology makes me nervous."

"I already have enough on my plate."

"I can't speak any other languages; how can I teach international students?"

These beliefs are all problem-based and not solution-based. They are *limiting* beliefs.

When you see a need, a lack, or a pain point, rather than focusing on the problem, look for a solution. Imagine how different your outcomes could be if you turned every stumbling block into a stepping-stone.

When I decided to teach chemistry online as a side job, my family had a lot to say.

"You don't have time; you already have your full-time commitment."

"You have three kids; where are you going to find the time?"

These are limiting beliefs. If you want to believe that you don't have time, you won't find the time. However, if you believe that you *can* manage your tasks and dedicate an hour or two every day to establishing your new endeavor, you *will* create the time. I believe that if you have a good reason—a good "why"—it will motivate you when things get difficult. In the next section of the book, I will talk a little more about finding your "why."

I found the time I needed to pursue my online teaching practice by setting aside two hours early in the morning, every morning, before my family woke up.

Another thing people said in response to my idea of teaching online was, "Where are you going to find students?"

I honestly didn't have the answer at the time, but I believed that students would come once I made the decision and started working toward my goal. There are billions of people worldwide who have access to the internet; among those, there are thousands of learners looking for a tutor.

When you make up your mind to pursue this idea, don't let the nay-sayers get you down. I know my family meant well when they posed their questions, but if I had let their doubts dissuade me, I'd still be drowning in debt and many students would not have had the advantage of being taught by me. We can't divorce ourselves from people who have negative mindsets and tell us all the reasons why this won't work, but we can choose to go ahead despite their negative beliefs.

Let us revisit some of the limiting, problem-based beliefs I mentioned earlier and see how we can turn them on their heads and turn them into solution-based ideas instead.

"I already teach full-time."

This is great because it means you are already in the swing of things. There's a quote by Elbert Hubbard that says, "If you want anything done, ask a busy person to do it." You already have the speed and the momentum; you are already moving forward, so taking on another role that runs parallel with your teaching won't mess up your stride. Plus, because you teach full-time, you probably have strong teaching skills. Use those skills to help more students.

"I'm still new to teaching."

This is not a problem. It's easier to branch out into new things before you get stuck in a rut. Plus, if you are a great teacher, it doesn't matter if you've been teaching for one year or ten years; the principle remains the same. Add value to your students' lives and help them improve their grades.

"Technology makes me nervous."

With the changes in teaching that the COVID-19 pandemic brought our way, we had to learn to use platforms such as Zoom to interact with our students. Don't let that experience go to waste. Once you get the hang of it, it will become second nature, just like standing in front of a class of learners. Most of the platforms are user-friendly, plus they have a helpful community of users who will gladly point you in the right direction if you get stuck. Growth may not be easy, but it is essential if you want to develop yourself. Pursuing new things leads to personal growth.

"I already have enough on my plate."

First, you will likely teach all your students in one Zoom meeting, so your teaching time will not exceed four hours per week. Second, as we will discover in the next section of the book, if it's important to you and you have a good reason to do it, you will be able to prioritize and make the time to do it. It can bring you greater fulfillment and put a few more dollars in your pocket.

"I can't speak any other languages; how can I teach international students?"

The international students I will be helping you reach are taught in English, which is why they are looking for

English-speaking tutors. Don't allow a limiting mindset to concoct excuses as to why you can't do this and why it won't work.

Find your "why" and use it to motivate you

"What we think determines what happens to us, so if we want to change our lives, we need to stretch our minds."

— WAYNE DYER

Focusing on the reason *why* we do things can help us when the going gets tough. Your "why" can be your motivator. My primary motivator is to make a positive impact on my students' lives. My secondary motivator, my reason "why," is to earn extra money to settle the six-figure debt I accumulated in student loans and borrowing money just to make ends meet.

Your "why" could be to save toward your child's college tuition, an international holiday, buying a car, a house, or simply just to make ends meet and not have to worry about the cost of living.

Your "why" will be a positive driving force because, on the days when lousy things happen, your "why" will help you carry on—especially in the beginning before your efforts start bringing in a steady financial reward. For example, some days it's not easy for me to get up two hours before everyone else. However, apart from the satisfaction I get from teaching my chemistry students online, I know that the income I receive for it has changed my financial standing and I am grateful for that. It motivates me. Monetary gain shouldn't be our primary goal; however, the money follows, so long as we provide valuable and helpful services.

You may be tired or not feeling well, a student may be rude to you, a parent may argue about your rate, or a technical glitch may cause you to miss a class. This is the real world. Things go wrong. Things like these examples may cause some people to quit. However, if you are sure of your "why" and have it dangling in front of you like a carrot on a stick, it can help you stay motivated.

So often, we as human beings *wish* things would change and *dream* of a brighter future. The truth is, wishes and dreams are not enough. There are so many variations of the following quote online that I'm not sure who to attribute it to, but the general consensus points to the author being Antoine de Saint-Exupéry: "A dream without a goal is a wish. A goal without a plan is just a dream."

Every business coach and mindset coach has adopted the essence of this quote and incorporated it as a catchphrase or as part of their program. Why? Because it's true and valid. Fairytale princesses have their dreams come true. In the real world, if you want your future to be different you have to change the way you're doing things now.

A dream written down with a date becomes a goal. A goal divided into steps becomes a plan. A plan backed by action makes your dream a reality.

— *GREG REID*

What is your dream?

A holiday abroad?

Putting your child (or yourself) through college without a student loan?

A new car?

A new home?

Freedom from financial pressure?

To help you turn your dream into a goal, start by following these simple steps:

Step 1: Write down your dream.

Step 2: Write down the date you want this dream to be realized.

Step 3: Write down the steps you must take to make it happen.

Step 4: Start acting on those steps.

Go into as much detail as possible when you write your dream and the subsequent steps. Don't just say, "I want to be debt-free by the end of next year" or, "I want to put my child through college after they graduate from high school." *How* are you going to achieve that?

For example, if you want to be debt-free, your dream-to-goal plan may look something like this:

Steps 1 and 2:

> I want to settle $6,300 credit card debt by X-month of Y-year, which is eighteen months away.

Step 3:

> To achieve this, I need to repay $350 per month.

To afford this, I need to earn an additional $350 per month.

To earn the additional money, I will tutor X students at Y dollars per hour for Z hours per month.

To become a tutor, I need to... (read on to find out!).

When planning the action steps required to achieve your goals, be realistic. If you owe hundreds of thousands of dollars, perhaps you can extend your goal to thirty-six months rather than eighteen.

We knew what we were getting into when we chose to become teachers. The pay isn't great, but we didn't let that dissuade us from pursuing our vocation. We know the irreplaceable impact teachers have on the futures of their learners. In the same way, when you look at international teaching as an opportunity, don't make it all about the money. Remember why you chose to teach in the first place and be thankful that your gift and talent can open a door for you to enrich the lives of others. The financial benefit is simply a result of the specialized service you can provide as an international tutor.

Embrace an attitude of giving and helping

When things go wrong, and when things go right, it is essential to have the right attitude. On the bad days, when students ask too much and demand more of your time, or when parents are critical of your teaching style and ask you to speed things up, a positive, optimistic, and loving mindset will help you overcome the worst.

Dr. Wayne Dyer says, "Attitude is everything, pick a good one!"[3] He also says, "If you change the way you look at things, the things you look at change."

Too often, we look on the outside for the solution to our problems. Would it surprise you to discover that the ability to solve most of your problems is within you? I'm sure you've heard the expression, "Your attitude determines your altitude." If we choose to adopt a positive attitude, it will result in a positive mindset. A positive mind thinks positive thoughts and expects positive outcomes.

Kathy and Tamryn are colleagues and friends. They teach at the same high school, their children are similar ages, and their husbands enjoy fishing together. They often laugh at how alike their lives are—they share similar struggles and dreams. Kathy saw one of my posts about becoming an international teacher and was immediately intrigued by the idea. She sent the link to Tamryn and called her soon after because she saw the potential opportunities. Sadly, Tamryn wasn't as enthusiastic. She kept telling Kathy that she didn't have the time, that her life was too busy, that there was no way she could find students. Kathy believed that if she could do it, so could Tamryn; but in reality, that is not true. Tamryn's mindset wasn't in the same positive place as Kathy's and as a result, no matter how hard Kathy tried she would not be able to convince her friend that this opportunity could work.

Here is a list of characteristics that match up with a positive mindset:

- **Integrity** Being honest, moral, and respectable rather than self-centered and falsehearted.
- **Optimism** The willingness to take a chance or put in an effort instead of presuming something is destined to fail before it's even begun.
- **Resilience**Bouncing back from disappointment, adversity, or failure rather than quitting.
- **Acceptance** Knowing things don't always go as planned, but not taking it personally and learning from the experience.
- **Gratitude** Consciously and actively appreciating all that is good in your life.

If you actively adopt these characteristics in your life, they could help you cultivate and maintain a positive mindset.

Think of each student as your own child who you want to see succeed. Think of your purpose in life. Remember your passion. Let the irritating comments go.

On the other side of the coin, when things are going well and your online teaching practice is a success, remain humble, thankful, and grateful.

It's a long-term commitment

I started with two students in my group lesson. It grew by word of mouth. After just one year, my class had grown to twenty-five students.

Expect students to join your class gradually. Have a long-term mentality. In the beginning, there's a lot of work that needs to be done and you may only have a few students. After a while, you will attract more and more students, but you won't need to do *more* work; you will have already laid the groundwork and established a system that works for you.

I have a system in place that makes payments and enrollments easy for the students and their parents, and I have delegated the administrative tasks to an employee. It's encouraging to know that things get easier with time.

Some teachers who have heard about my teaching model say, "But this will take time."

Yes, it may take several months to see results. That's one thing we've all been given an equal portion of: We all have twenty-four hours a day. However, people use their given time differently. Time passes whether you use it constructively or not.

I like to use the analogy of a brick-and-mortar building when I think of my online teaching model. Firstly, the building takes time to construct, especially the foundation, in the same way that your online business will not happen overnight. But, once it's built, it will stand for years. Secondly, as opposed to a physical building, which takes a substantial financial investment whether you are building from scratch or buying one already built for investment purposes, my international teaching idea requires minimal capital outlay.

For example, if you buy an apartment with the idea of renting it out for extra income, you need capital to invest in the apartment initially and it could take years before you break even, and then even longer before you start making a profit. Again, I speak from experience: I tried buying and selling to make extra money, and it ended up costing me a lot more than I made. I spent thousands of dollars on stock that sat in my garage and haunted me. Then, I had to spend a lot of precious time and effort trying to sell it.

Yes, this online teaching business takes time—but time and a little effort are really all it takes.

Remember, demand equals opportunity

Being an international, online teacher is the same as being a teacher in a brick-and-mortar classroom: You are meeting a need. Students need to be educated. You should never feel guilty, greedy, or awkward about providing a service for a fee. In fact, everyone who has a job or provides a service is meeting a need—we're all selling our time, skills, and expertise.

Unfortunately, for whatever reason, teachers don't earn what other college graduates in comparable positions earn. But that doesn't mean our jobs are less important or that we are less valuable. And it definitely doesn't mean that we should sell ourselves short when we offer our services as tutors or online teachers over and above our day jobs.

As I detailed earlier, there is a shortage of teachers worldwide. This shortage, coupled with increasing pressure amongst students to get excellent grades, has led to an increased demand for good tutors. Add to this the advent of modern technology; students from non-English countries are turning to online offerings seeking English-speaking teachers around the world to help them excel in all their subjects in an English curriculum.

I often have parents asking me for recommendations for teachers in other subjects or other levels; I only teach a specific curriculum in chemistry. When people ask, I give them lists of names, but sometimes the parents come back and say they have tried so-and-so and they are not satisfied. Either the student's performance didn't improve, or the teacher speaks poor English. My immediate reaction when I hear things like this is, "I want to solve this problem. I want to connect great teachers to hard-working, appreciative students." That was the seed idea behind writing this book.

High school is high stakes. Students' scores have a huge impact on their future. It's a big deal. So much emphasis is placed on these few years of the student's life. Parents pay more attention and invest more of their time, energy, and money in the hope that their children will get the grades they need to go to college or university and get a degree.

These factors all work together to create a demand and, if you're willing, you can (and should) turn that demand into an opportunity.

What are your expectations?

I didn't have *big* expectations, but I had *positive* ones. It took me a year to go from two to five and then to twenty-five students. You can attain better results in a shorter time because I'm sharing how *I* did it and taking the guesswork out of the equation for you.

I often get asked, "How much can I expect to make?"

That's a difficult question to answer. Everyone is different. It depends on a lot of things, including how dedicated you are.

Don't be concerned if you start with only a few students. Work well and give them your best. When their grades improve, the magic of "word of mouth" will happen. Once your students' grades improve, other parents will ask them to provide the list of teachers they studied with. When your name hits that list, you will have many students wanting to enroll in your classes.

CHAPTER 1 IN A NUTSHELL

Henry Ford once said, *"Whether you think you can, or you think you can't—you're right."*

I hope I've convinced you that there is a demand for the skills you possess. There are students in other countries crying out for good English-speaking teachers to help them get the grades they need.

There are lots of things teachers can do to earn extra money—we're innovative. However, not many of those ideas require zero capital start-up.

You already possess the skill set; add to that the right mindset and you are one step away from becoming a successful international teacher. So, what is the next step? Stick with me as we delve into Chapters 2 and 3. The next two chapters are full of detailed and valuable information about the curriculum and exams associated with tutoring international students. If, at first, some of the terminologies are difficult to grasp, don't worry. Everything will become clear as we make our way through the book.

GETTING STARTED

"The secret to getting ahead is getting started."

— *MARK TWAIN*

"Start" is a little word that carries a lot of weight. It is the difference between staying in the same place, year after year, or heading in a new direction.

Isn't life a funny thing? Just as you're about to take an important step, something comes up. Those "some-things" are critical sometimes, but if you're honest, sometimes they are time-wasters and energy-sappers.

There has to come a point when you decide to go for it, regardless of what life sends your way, or you'll be looking back one year, two years, or five years from now and thinking, "If only I had...."

Do you have a dream? Have you written it down and turned it into a goal with a date? Have you divided your goal into steps to make it a plan? Now you need to "action" (act on) your plan to make it a reality. Quite simply—you need to take the first step!

Nothing will change until you start.

I kicked off this chapter with a quote by Mark Twain; allow me the liberty to expand on it. "The secret to getting ahead is getting started"—true. But the secret to getting started is breaking big tasks into small manageable steps, and then taking action on the first one.

In this case, your first step is getting to know the curriculum.

GETTING TO GRIPS WITH THE CURRICULUM

Your long-term goal is not to teach one-on-one, but to a *group* of students. For obvious reasons, one-on-one means there is a cap on your income because you only have twenty-four hours in a day. Teaching a group of students at the same time means you can have an "unlimited" number of students in your live two-hour session. I say "unlimited" but, in reality, you should only have as many students as you can keep tabs on. If you take on so many students that you don't have the time to provide personalized feedback and follow-up, you may lose some students; their parents are looking for the results that come with having a hands-on tutor.

In Chapter 6, we will look into recording your lessons and selling recorded courses. When you do this, you no longer earn money in exchange for your time; you are earning money for your expertise.

When you teach international students, you will have to familiarize yourself with their curriculum. Apart from deciding on the curriculum, you will also have to decide beforehand what grade level you want to teach. There is potential to specialize in one grade level in one subject. As I mentioned in Chapter 1, I only teach Ordinary Level Chemistry. There is a demand for chemistry teachers in all the other levels and for English-speaking teachers specifically in all subjects, not just in chemistry.

International students study a variety of curricula. Some study the American system, and others choose to study the British system. The British system is called the IGCSE—the International General Certificate for Secondary Education. There is an enormous demand for teachers who are willing to teach this curriculum.

The IGCSE curriculum

I began teaching IGCSE chemistry online in 2019. I'm going to share with you all the information you need to make an informed decision about the IGCSE curriculum. At first, some of the terms may be unfamiliar to you, but don't worry about that; it will make complete sense after I've explained everything.

The history of the IGSCE curriculum

The IGCSE is a globally recognized qualification, formed in 1988.[1] It is a comprehensive two-year program with final examinations offered twice a year, in May and November.

Assessment Levels

In the International Assessment curriculum, the subjects are offered at three different levels:

O-Level

The Ordinary Level, or O-Level, is the lowest level. The GCSE is now the predominant course and exam taken for sixteen-year-olds in the UK, the equivalent of US Grade 10. Internationally, the IGCSE O-Level exams are taken generally in Grade 10 or 11 (depending on the school).

AS-Level

The Advanced Supplementary Level, or AS-Level, is one level higher than the standard GCSE. One AS-Level equates to half the syllabus content of the A-Level, and it is taught in Grade 11 in most international schools. In the UK, this is often year one of two at what they term "sixth-form" college. It can be taken as a standalone qualification or as a precursor to the A-Level.

A-Level

The Advanced Level, or A-Level, is the most difficult level and is worth the most credits. In international schools, the A-Level is taught either as the subsequent, second part of a qualification after AS-Levels, to achieve a full A-Level, or alternatively, linearly across Grades 11 and 12 as a standalone qualification, with all exams sat in Grade 12.

With the Cambridge Assessment International Education curricula, learners can choose from a range of assessment options when it comes to AS- and A-Level Assessments.

1. Take the Cambridge International AS-Level

only: The syllabus contains half the content of the Cambridge International A-Level.

2. Choose a staggered assessment route: Take the Cambridge International AS-Level in one examination series and complete the final Cambridge International A-Level in a subsequent series. AS-Level grades can be carried forward to a full A-Level twice within a thirteen-month period.

3. Take all Cambridge International A-Level course papers in the same examination session, usually at the end of the course.

There are differences in subject requirements from country to country. In most countries, students are required to complete a number of Ordinary Level subjects (usually five to eight subjects) and a fewer number of Advanced Level subjects (usually two to four subjects).

There is a considerable gap in the market for teachers at AS-Level and A-Level. The fact that each subject is divided into three levels confirms that there is a demand for teachers in each subject across all three levels.

What is the difference between IGCSE and GCSE?

Firstly, what is GCSE?

GCSE means General Certificate of Secondary Education. It is the school qualification taken by UK students at the age of sixteen.

The most significant difference between the UK GCSE and the IGCSE is that the IGCSE's curriculum has more international content. For example, the UK GCSE in geography will focus on maps and climate studies from the UK, while the IGCSE in geography will include maps and climate studies from global regions. The IGCSE also offers a broader range of subjects, particularly languages. Put simply, the IGCSE is founded in the GSCE curriculum but made more suitable for international students, thus adding the "I" in the acronym. Throughout this book, I will only discuss the IGCSE (not the GCSE), because that's where my experience lies, and what I teach my international students.

IGCSE exam boards

Exam boards are organizations that offer qualifications to students. It is up to the exam board to produce exam papers, mark the exams, and award the grade.

Under the IGCSE umbrella, there are three exam boards:[2]

1. Cambridge IGCSE,

2. Pearson Edexcel International GCSE, and

3. OxfordAQA International GCSE

All of the boards offer qualifications that are internationally recognized and accepted by colleges and universities around the world.

How does IGCSE compare to an American high school diploma?

According to US colleges and universities, IGCSE grades are normally regarded as the equivalent of a US high school diploma. Many schools regard A-Levels as a rough equivalent of US Grade 11 plus a little more. Also, A-Levels can sometimes count for US university credit: Usually, one A-Level can equal three undergraduate credits.

How does the IGCSE compare to other programs?

The IGCSE offers a wide range of subjects (over seventy) and encourages high academic standards. Assessments are not limited to written papers; rather, they include a variety of oral and listening tests.

What is the difference between the Extended and Core curricula?

Most subjects offer a choice between Extended curriculum and Core curriculum. The Core curriculum provides a complete overview of the subject. It is suitable for learners who are expected to achieve grades C to G. The Extended curriculum offers specialization in the subject. It allows for higher education or professional training.[3] The Extended curriculum includes extra topics, covered in greater depth, in addition to the Core curriculum. It is designed for students who are expected to achieve grades A+ to C because it is more challenging.

Students can choose different levels of curriculum in their various subjects; they don't have to study all their subjects in the Core or Extended curriculum but can mix and match.

Since your international students will be aiming for straight A+s, they will be on the Extended curriculum; thus, your goal is to teach it.

Why do students choose the IGCSE curriculum?

The IGCSE is based on the GCSE (the British curriculum), but it has been adapted for a more international student body. Exams are graded through the exam board chosen by the school or the student.

The IGSCE curriculum is popular because it offers a large variety of subjects and it aims to be as inclusive as possible of learners from different linguistic backgrounds. Here are some of the advantages offered by the IGCSE curriculum:

- IGCSE qualifications are accepted by over 1,900 institutions across eighty-one countries.
- The IGCSE is an immensely rich program designed to prepare students for further study.
- The IGCSE board ensures that students get the utmost attention regarding their learning.
- They are famous for using different teaching and learning practices designed to help students learn the lessons in the most effective ways.
- The curriculum encourages students to investigate different issues, ask questions, and analyze what will help with their understanding.
- They use assessments that are reliable and trusted.
- The assessments are fair and flexible.
- They are focused on conceptual learning and promote the overall development of higher order thinking skills among students.
- If you're sending your child to an IGCSE school, you ensure that your child is exposed to a well-built and organized curriculum.
- The exam boards carry international recognition, which can benefit the student's career.

How many students are studying the International GCSE curriculum?

More than 10,000 schools across 160 countries offer International GCSE programs and qualifications. The Cambridge IGCSE is the most common, taken in more than 4,500 schools in over 140 countries. Cambridge O-Levels are taught in over fifty countries. The Cambridge International AS- and A-Levels (a higher-level qualification, taken at age eighteen in the UK) have more than 530,000 subject entries each year in over 130 countries.

Cambridge offers the IGCSE O Level, in addition to the higher-level qualifications, AS-Level, and A-Level courses.[4]

In total, every year, nearly a million learners prepare for their future with an education in the Cambridge IGCSE, which is a non-profit organization and part of the world-renowned University of Cambridge. I will cover some of the basic information about each of the three IGCSE exam boards, starting with Cambridge, the most popular.

1. Cambridge IGCSE

The Cambridge IGCSE curriculum offers different routes for learners including those whose first language is not English, which is one of the reasons why it is popular amongst the schools in the countries where my students reside.

Cambridge IGCSE offers over seventy subjects including thirty languages, and schools can offer them in any combination.[5]

To follow is an alphabetical list of most subjects offered by Cambridge IGCSE and their corresponding subject codes. Subject codes are a 4-digit number unique to each subject:[6]

TABLE 1

Accounting* 0452 0985	Afrikaans– Second Language 0548	Agriculture 0600	Arabic–First Language * 0508 7184	Arabic–Foreign Language 0544
Art and Design* 0400 0989	Bahasa Indonesia 0538	Biology* 0610 0970	Business Studies* 0450 0986	Chemistry* 0620 0971
Chinese–First Language 0509	Chinese– Second Language 0523	Chinese (Mandarin)– Foreign Language 0547	Computer Science* 0478 0984	Design and Technology* 0445 0979
Drama* 0411 0994	Dutch–Foreign Language 0515	Economics* 0455 0987	English–First Language * 0500 0990	English–First Language (US) 0524

English–Literature (US) 0427	English–Literature in English* 0475 0992	English (Additional Language) 0472 0772	English–Second Language (Count-in Speaking) * 0511 0991	English–Second Language (Speaking Endorsement) * 0510 0993
Enterprise 0454	Environmental Management 0680	Food and Nutrition 0648	French–First Language* 0501	French–Foreign Language 0520 7156
Geography* 0460 0976	German–First Language * 0505	German–Foreign Language 0525 7159	Global Perspectives 0457	Greek–Foreign Language 0543
Hindi–Second Language 0549	History* 0470 0977	History–American (US) 0409	Indonesian–Foreign Language 0545	Information and Communication Technology* 0417 0983
IsiZulu–Second Language 0531	Islamiyat 0493	Italian–Foreign Language 0535	Italian 7164	Japanese–Foreign Language 0519
Korean–First Language 0521	Latin 0480	Malay–First Language 0696	Malay–Foreign Language 0546	Marine Science 0697
Mathematics* 0580 0980	Mathematics–Additional 0606	Mathematics–Additional (US) 0459	Mathematics–International 0607	Mathematics (US) 0444
Music * 0410 0978	Pakistan Studies 0448	Physical Education* 0413 0995	Physical Science 0652	Physics* 0625 0972
Portuguese–First Language 0504	Portuguese–Foreign Language 0540	Religious Studies 0490	Russian–First Language 0516	Sanskrit 0499
Science–Combined 0653	Sciences–Co-ordinated* 0654 0973	Sociology 0495	Spanish–First Language* 0502	Spanish–Foreign Language 0530 7160
Spanish–Literature 0488	Swahili 0262	Thai–First Language 0518	Travel and Tourism 0471	Turkish–First Language 0513
Urdu–Second Language 0539	World Literature 0408			

Please Note Subjects marked with the * have two grading options: a letter grade or a number grade. Subjects without the * use the letter grading system only.

Other than the difference in the grading system, the syllabus is the same.

Cambridge IGCSE Grading System

Currently, the IGCSE uses a letter-based grading system, and in some subjects, there is the option to choose a number-based grading system, which is used by most UK schools.[7]

The following table illustrates how the letter-based and number-based grades compare with one another:

TABLE 2

Letter	Number
A*	9
A	8
	7
B	6
	5
C	4
D	3
E	2
F	
G	1
U	U

A* (pronounced "A-star") is also known as A+. In the numerical-grading system, 9 is the highest and 1 is the lowest. In both systems, "U" means "ungraded." At the time of writing this book, the numerical system is, in my opinion, better for the student as I will explain below.

The difference between letter and number grades

The advantage of letter grades is that students and parents are accustomed to them, so they know immediately how to interpret them.

The disadvantages apply more to the person who is doing the grading. It's tricky to choose how to mark an assignment that's borderline between two letter grades. How do you record an A-/B+ in a spreadsheet?

The advantages of using number grades:

- Numbers work better than letters in a spreadsheet formula, making record keeping easier.
- A bit more fine-tuning is possible when it comes to assigning and recording borderline grades.

Let's now look at the breakdown of some of the IGCSE assessments that take place in three example subjects— English, Combined Sciences, and Math:

O-Level English Language

Candidates for O-Level English Language must take two compulsory components: Paper 1 and Paper 2.

Paper 1—Writing

Students have to answer two questions: one compulsory question in Section 1 and one chosen question from Section 2.

Section 1: Directed Writing

Section 2: Composition, where students choose one writing task from a choice of five essay titles.

Duration: 1 hour 30 minutes

Marks: 60

Weighting: 50% of O-Level

Paper 2—Reading

Students answer all of the questions in both sections.

Section 1: Reading for ideas

Section 2: Reading for meaning

Duration: 1 hour 45 minutes

Marks: 50

Weighting: 50% of O-Level

AS-Level and A-Level English Language

Candidates for AS- and A-Level English Language must take four assessments, Papers 1 to 4.

Paper 1—Reading

Students answer two compulsory questions.

Duration: 2 hours 15 minutes

Marks: 50

Weighting: 50% of AS-Level and 25% of A-Level

Paper 2—Writing

Students answer two questions: one compulsory question and one chosen question from a choice of three.

Duration: 2 hours

Marks: 50

Weighting: 50% of AS-Level and 25% of A-Level

Paper 3—Language Analysis

Students answer two compulsory questions.

Duration: 2 hours 15 minutes

Marks: 50

Weighting: 25% of A-Level

Paper 4—Language Topics

Students answer two compulsory questions.

Duration: 2 hours 15 minutes

Marks: 50

Weighting: 25% of A-Level

O-Level Combined Science

For O-Level Combined Science, students complete two assessments.

Paper 1—Multiple Choice

Forty compulsory multiple-choice questions taken from biology, physics, and chemistry.

Duration: 1 hour

Marks: 40

Weighting: 29% of O-Level

Paper 2—Theory

Compulsory, structured questions taken from biology, physics, and chemistry.

Duration: 2 hours 15 minutes

Weighting: 71% of O-Level

O-Level Mathematics

O-Level Math can be studied at Core level or Extended level, as I detailed earlier. International Extended level students are required to take Paper 2 and Paper 4.

Paper 2

Short-answer questions based on the Extended curriculum.

Duration: 1 hour 30 minutes

Marks: 70

Weighting: 35% of O-Level

Paper 4

Structured questions based on the Extended curriculum.

Duration: 2 hours 30 minutes

Marks: 130

Weighting: 65% of O-Level

AS-Level and A-Level Mathematics

Candidates for AS-Level Math who do not wish to progress to A-Level will only take Paper 1 and Paper 2. AS-Level students who want to progress to A-Level will also take Paper 4 and Paper 5. A-Level candidates will take Paper 1, Paper 3, Paper 4, Paper 5, and Paper 6.

Paper 1—Pure Mathematics 1

Students answer ten to twelve structured questions based on Pure Mathematics 1 subject content.

Duration: 1 hour 50 minutes

Marks: 75

Weighting: 60% of AS-Level and 30% of A-Level

Compulsory for AS-Level and A-Level

Paper 2—Pure Mathematics 2

Students answer six to eight structured questions based on Pure Mathematics 2 subject content.

Duration: 1 hour 15 minutes

Marks: 50

Weighting: 40% of AS-Level

Offered only as part of AS-Level

Paper 3—Pure Mathematics 3

Students answer nine to eleven structured questions based on Pure Mathematics 3 subject content.

Duration: 1 hour 50 minutes

Marks: 75

Weighting: 30% of A-Level

Compulsory for A-Level

Paper 4—Mechanics

Students answer six to eight structured questions based on Mechanics subject content.

Duration: 1 hour 15 minutes

Marks: 50

Weighting: 40% of AS-Level and 20% of A-Level

Offered as part of AS-Level or A-Level

Paper 5—Probability and Statistics 1

Students answer six to eight structured questions based on the probability and Statistics 1 subject content.

Duration: 1 hour 15 minutes

Marks: 50

Weighting: 40% of AS-Level and 20% of A-Level

Compulsory for A-Level

Paper 6—Probability and Statistics 2

Students answer six to eight structured questions based on the Probability and Statistics 1 subject content.

Duration: 1 hour 15 minutes

Marks: 50

Weighting: 20% of A-Level

Offered as part of A-Level only

I have described the assessment of just three subjects; however, there are many more subjects that are in high demand. To view the most recent assessment information about all IGCSE subjects, visit cambridgeinternational.org.

2. Pearson Edexcel International GCSE

Pearson Edexcel was previously known as Edexcel IGCSE and is now known as Edexcel International GCSE. It is equivalent to the Cambridge IGCSE qualification.

Edexcel International GCSE's curriculum is designed to cover academic content and assessment that will enable successful advancement for international learners.

To follow is an alphabetical list of most subjects offered by Pearson Edexcel International GCSE:[8]

TABLE 3

Art, Design, and Media	Beauty Therapy and Hairdressing	Business, Administration, and Law	Childcare	Citizenship
Cleaning	Computer Science and ICT	Construction, Planning, and the Built Environment	Design and Technology	Drama, Theatre, and Performing Arts
Economics	Education and Training	Energy and Utilities	Engineering	English
Esports	Finance and Accounting	First Aid	Food Manufacturing	Funeral Services
General Studies	Geography	Health and Social Care	History	Home Economics
Hospitality and Catering	Land-Based	Languages	Manufacturing Technologies	Maths and Statistics
Medicine and Dentistry	Music	Physical Education and Sport	Politics	Property and Housing
Public Services	Religious Studies	Retailing and Wholesaling	Science	Security
Textiles and Apparel Manufacturing	Transportation, Operations, and Maintenance	Travel and Tourism	Warehousing and Distribution	

3. OxfordAQA International GCSE

OxfordAQA International GCSE focuses on eight main subjects. They are listed below, along with the sub-categories that fall under the main subject:[9]

TABLE 4

Main Subject	Sub-Categories of the Main Subject
Mathematics	Mathematics Further Mathematics
Science	Physics Chemistry Biology Combined Science
English	English Language English Literature
Business	Not applicable
Computer Science	Not applicable
Geography	Not applicable
Psychology	Not applicable
Economics	Not applicable

OxfordAQA International GCSE qualifications are a research-based combination of UK specifications, subject matter, and resources that enhance the learning experience for international students.

CHAPTER 2 IN A NUTSHELL

Chapter 2 had us jumping in with both feet. First, we got to grips with the IGCSE curriculum, including the history, how it compares to other curricula, and why international students choose IGCSE. We also investigated the three IGCSE exam boards and looked at the subjects that each of them offers. Finally, we had a look at the grading systems and assessments.

Chapter 3 is divided into two parts. Part 1 is dedicated to showing you the value of past exam papers. Part 2 offers a step-by-step guide to enrolling in a Cambridge IGSCE marking workshop and all the information you'll need regarding Pearson Edexcel and OxfordAQA workshops and webinars.

Scan the QR code to watch this short training video called: Downloading Teaching Resources.

3

PREPARING STUDENTS FOR EXAMS

"Learn from the past. Prepare for the future. Live in the present."

— *THOMAS S. MONSON*

As a teacher, I'm sure you are aware of the importance of your students doing well in their assessments and exams. For some students, specifically those you will be aiming to teach online, exam results will determine their futures to a huge degree (pardon the pun).

In essence, your student's grades will determine which university or college they go to after graduating from high school. And, if your student's grades improve under your tutorship, it means you will have a long list of students wanting to join your classes.

With this in mind, chapter three aims to highlight the value of past papers in your lessons and as a resource tool in your teaching practice. I also aim to demonstrate how you can best equip yourself by signing up for a marking workshop and other relevant webinars.

PART 1: THE VALUE OF PAST EXAM PAPERS

The past is a good place to learn from; after all, hindsight is a good teacher. This idiom appropriately describes the value of past exam papers.

Past exam papers are available for free online. Each exam board publishes its exams a few months after they are administered to exam takers. These exams are ideal for students to practice on; I'm sure many teachers already know of the particular benefit of past papers.

However, there is more that can be done with past papers than just practicing for exams, and that's what I aim to detail in this part of the chapter.

Firstly, let's look at where you can find the past papers.

A quick internet search for "Cambridge IGCSE past papers" will get you what you're looking for: you should see a result for "Past Papers | Cambridge IGCSE | GCE Guide."[1] It's that easy. Once you click the link, you can scroll down the page and click on O-Levels, IGCSE, or AS- & A-Levels—whichever is applicable for you.

You will then see a list of all subjects and their corresponding subject codes, like the list I presented in Table 1. Click on the subject you're teaching: I'm going to use IGCSE Chemistry 0620 as my example.

When I clicked on Chemistry, a new page opened with folders named after the year the exam took place: in this instance, 2002 until 2021. I selected 2015 for the sake of this example and the page that opened offered me twenty-two PDF files under June and another twenty-two files under November. This is because Cambridge IGCSE exams occur twice a year: June and November. These PDFs include eight exam papers for each session, plus the multiple-choice answer sheets and the relevant mark scheme. I will explain the use of the mark scheme in detail in Part 2 of this chapter.

For interest's sake, I clicked on English. Once again, there were folders named from 2002 to 2021. I clicked on 2015 and found fifteen PDF files under June and another fifteen under November. These included four question papers with their corresponding answers and mark scheme.

Try it! It's incredible to see the extent of this resource that is at your fingertips. Choose any subject, select a year, and voila—past papers galore.

In 2009 and the years prior, there are fewer past exam papers than from 2010 onward. In 2010, Cambridge introduced different exam versions for separate regions where previously it had been one exam for the whole world. These different exams are called variants. The reason for creating these variants was due to the different time zones. For example, Indonesia is five hours ahead of Egypt. Cambridge divided the countries that write their exams into six administrative time zones. They then issue three variants of each exam amongst these different zones. This way, they can prevent students in the eastern parts of the world, who write their exams first, from contacting friends in more western countries to tell them what to expect in the exam.

The fact that there are now three variants for each exam is handy because it means that, since 2010, our past paper resources have tripled!

Questions in past papers do not often repeat themselves. The exam boards keep tweaking their questions and getting creative. And the curriculum doesn't change much, so even though I'm teaching the most recent syllabus, exams from 2002 are still applicable.

Now that you know where to find these past papers, let's discuss how we can use them in our lessons.

What I found to be a common problem in chemistry—and I'm sure it's the same with other subjects—was once my students had finished learning Chapter 1, they wanted to practice everything to do with Chapter 1. Unfortunately for them, all they can find on the internet is a bunch of past papers that include mixed questions from all the chapters. The question papers do not specify which question belongs to which chapter.

So, I look at all the past papers, collect all the questions related to Chapter 1, and put them in one document. Armed with this resource, I can teach Chapter 1 to my students and then give them all the questions related to that chapter. This allows my students to learn, study, and practice one chapter at a time.

I saw this as an opportunity to sort through and find all the questions that belonged to Chapter 1 and put them in one document. I then created a second document with the questions and the answers. I now have two separate documents that I can use as resources for the work covered in Chapter 1. The first document really helps students who want to study Chapter 1 and have a variety of questions to practice. The second document provides my students with the ideal answers for review.

Although it can take some time to put together a document like this, it doesn't have to be complicated. I simply took a screenshot, cropped the question, and pasted it into a new text document. I then referred to the mark sheet to see what Cambridge says is an acceptable answer and wrote my answer as the ideal answer. I duplicated this process with all the questions relevant to Chapter 1 from all the past papers. If you want to do this process in a much shorter time, gather questions from the last three years only, instead of all past papers available.

Past papers as a resource tool

While I'm scouring the past papers for questions relating to Chapter 1, I keep a lookout for questions from the other chapters. It's as simple as taking a screenshot, cropping the question, and pasting it into an appropriately named document.

To make my life easy and help me find my documents quickly, I name the files after the chapter and then differentiate between "questions only" (Q), and "questions and answers" (QA). For example Chapter 1 Q, Chapter 1 QA, Chapter 2 Q, Chapter 2 QA, etc. If you are teaching more than one subject or more than one level, be sure to include that information in the file name too, or you may become flummoxed by your own filing system.

In the beginning, while I was establishing my credibility as an online teacher on various social media platforms, I shared my Chapter 1 documents to add free value for those on the social media groups. Chapter 4 of this book will explain in more detail how you can use social media groups and your past paper resources to establish yourself as a great teacher. Doing so will make it easier for you to start your online classes.

The documents I created for the other chapters are not distributed as free value; they are available on my website for a small fee.[2] Because parents and students appreciated that the document was well organized and aided them in their practice, they happily purchased materials for the remaining chapters. I do, however, provide everything to students who enroll in my year-long course.

I feel I must take the time to remind you that it is perfectly acceptable and even advisable to offer some of your resources as free value, while others should be *sold* and *not* given away. Why do I say this? You are an expert in your field. Your time is valuable. It may not be difficult, but it is time-consuming to sort through all the past papers to find questions relevant to the various chapters and put them all in their respective documents. And then, creating the question-and-answer document will take that much more time and effort on your part.

You deserve to be paid for your time and expertise. Understanding that your time has value and that these documents are a valuable resource that parents are willing to pay for should help you overcome any thoughts you may be harboring of simply giving all of your resources away for free.

PART 2: ENROLLING IN A MARKING WORKSHOP

I would highly recommend for teachers to enroll in a marking workshop with Cambridge IGCSE, Pearson Edexcel, or OxfordAQA—whichever examination board you choose to go with.

This workshop trains you on how to mark (grade) exam papers. The information you glean from learning how to grade exams is exactly what you need to help teach your students to achieve the best possible exam results. For example, armed with the relevant exam grading information, you can advise your students that if they want to score full marks for a specific question, they should mention "these key words" or make "these points."

Completing a marking (grading) workshop helps you know exactly how to prepare your students for exams, which is the most important aspect of your role as an online teacher. In addition, an improvement in their results is the best advertisement you could possibly hope for when it comes to word-of-mouth advertising for your practice.

I took one of the Cambridge marking workshops because I teach the Cambridge curriculum. During the course, we practiced marking actual student exams that had been scanned from the various countries where the students sat the exam. This gives you a real feel for the international side of teaching. You may be pleasantly surprised to see the student's grasp of the English language even though they are not from English-speaking countries.

The mark scheme

What we call "grading" papers in the US is known as "marking" papers in the UK education system. The mark scheme is the guide to the grader. For example, it tells the grader, "These are the terms or concepts we're looking for. If you're grading this question, you want to make sure the student mentions XYZ." Another example of what the workshop teaches is, "What if the student writes something else? Can marks still be awarded?"

The multiple-choice papers are easy to mark because the answer is either A, B, C, or D. Apart from multiple-choice, students also write various short-answer questions and, for the science papers, there is an "alternative to practice" paper which asks the student to plan an experiment, describe the observations of an experiment, or sketch a graph. This will vary slightly from subject to subject, but you will be able to find more information on the various exams for each subject, as I explained in Chapter 2, on the Cambridge website.

The workshop allows teachers to discuss and compare how they graded each paper, which I found especially helpful. You will be taught where to deduct points and where to award points. Ultimately, taking this workshop will equip you to help your students best prepare for their exams.

How to sign up for the Cambridge IGCSE Marking Workshop

In the next section of the book, I will give you a step-by-step guide to signing up for a marking workshop with Cambridge IGCSE (all the links are in the reference section at the end of the book), since this is the one I'm most familiar with.

But first, here are some points of interest regarding the workshop:

- The workshop takes place online and, in some areas, in person. To find out if there are in-person workshops in your area, visit the Online Marking Workshops page on the Cambridge International website.[3]
- The training takes place in English.
- The workshop is recommended for teachers who will teach a Cambridge curriculum for at least one exam cycle or one year.
- You will work with recently submitted exams from real students—not mock exam papers.
- There are two workshops. One for coursework only, the "Coursework Workshop," and another for exams called a "Marking Workshop."
- Workshops each last for three weeks and focus on the following:

Week 1—Grading student papers
Week 2—Grading standardization
Week 3—Reviewing your grading and an open Q&A session with other teachers

- You will spend three to four hours per week, a total of nine hours, across the three weeks of the workshop.
- Activities and discussions are group-based.
- We recommend that you access the course

material daily; however, you may do so at a time that suits you.

- Clear guidelines are provided so that you know in advance which days to carry out which activities.
- You will receive a certificate of attendance when you complete key activities each week and engage in group discussions.
- Bookings are limited to twenty-five participants per session.
- The workshops run six times per year: February, March, April, September, October, and November.
- There is a 20 percent discount for those who book early—so be sure to take advantage of this.
- The subjects fall under four subsections: Cambridge IGCSE, Cambridge O-Level, Cambridge International AS-Level, and Cambridge International A- & AS-Level.
- All information can be found on the Cambridge International help pages under the training section.[4]

Alright, let's get down to signing up for that workshop!

Step 1: You can go to Cambridge's website and search for the marking workshops link, or you can let your search engine (for example, Google) do the work for you. I simply typed "sign up for Cambridge IGCSE marking workshop" into my search box and the first search result at the top of the page was "Online Marking Workshops—Cambridge International."

Step 2: Click on the "Online Marking Workshops—Cambridge International" link and you'll land on the Online Marking Workshop page.[5]

Step 3: Scroll down past all the information to the bottom where you will find a list of subjects with their corresponding subject codes. Remember, if there are two codes, it means that that subject has the choice of two grading systems: letters or numbers.

Step 4: Select the appropriate options. For this example, I chose the first subject on the Cambridge IGCSE list: Accounting.

Step 5: A drop-down menu opened, giving me a choice between workshops in two separate months. Incidentally, the options I was given were seven and eight months away, which means that if you want to book one of these workshops, the sooner you do so, the better.

Step 6: Click the "Book" button next to the marking workshop you want to do.

Step 7: A new window will open that displays the course code as well as the start and end dates of the course, the course times, and the early bird fee—which at the time of writing this book was £80, roughly $110 (the exact figure will depend on the exchange rate).

Step 8: Read the overview information. It includes points like the ones I listed in the bullets above but also includes additional information:

- The course tutor is a subject matter expert and will be available to answer questions regarding the syllabus.
- Teamwork and reflection are imperative to learning how to grade papers effectively.
- Group activities will be monitored and overseen by an experienced Cambridge tutor.
- By the end of the course, you will be familiar with what examiners are looking for.
- This additional insight will enable you to focus your classroom activities on the areas where your learners need to improve.

Step 9: Click on the "Add to cart" button.

Step 10: Confirm your dates by looking at the calendar that appears on the next page. The workshop includes weekends, so be sure you have no plans that will prevent you from participating in the workshop and, while you're at it, block off those dates on your personal calendar.

Step 11: Click on the "My cart (1 Item)" icon.

Step 12: You have another opportunity to review the calendar and make sure you have selected the right subject (by confirming that the subject code corresponds to yours) before you click on the "Confirm Booking" button. Or you can click on the "Remove" button if you need to change to another date or choose a different subject.

Step 13: You will be prompted to log in to your account with your email and password. If you do not have an account, you can click on the "Create account" button. For the sake of this exercise, I will assume you don't have an account; the next few steps will help you create an account.

Step 14: Click the "Create account" button.

Step 15: You will be prompted to enter your email address and confirm your email. And you will be prompted to enter a password and confirm your password. Once you have entered your email and password, click the "Next" button.

Step 16: You will be asked to tick the consent box, confirming that you have read the Data Protection and Privacy Statement. Then click the "Next" button.

Step 17: You will be required to complete a form that includes your title, name*, email*, email verification*, phone number, country*, center number, and job title* —items marked with an asterisk are mandatory.

The "Job Title" box opens a drop-down menu where you can choose between teacher, exam officer, middle leader (head of department, head of year, or senior teacher), senior leader (principal, head of school, director, deputy principal), non-teaching staff, or other.

Please note: The details provided during booking must be the details of the person attending the course.

Once you have filled in the information, select whether you want to receive email notifications about future Cambridge International events by ticking the relevant option.

Step 18: Tick the "I consent" box if you would not mind being invited to participate in research and feedback regarding Cambridge services, qualifications, and support materials. Once you have ticked all the right boxes, you can click the "Back" or "Next" button. If you are happy with your details and the workshop you have chosen, click "Next."

Step 19: Enter your payment details. There is an option to send the invoice to a center or organization, or if you leave this part out, the invoice will be emailed to the address you filled in while completing the form. You will also be given an opportunity to fill in a discount code, should you have one. Once you have selected if you want to pay in GBP, EUR, or USD, or you have selected the option to send the invoice to a center, you will click on the "Confirm" button.

Step 20: A window will pop up asking if you would like to continue. If you'd like to change anything, click "No." However, if you are happy with the information you have entered, and you're sure you have selected the right subject workshop and the right workshop dates, click on the "Yes" button.

Congratulations! You are one step closer to becoming a Marking Workshop certified teacher who will help students prepare for their exams and get the grades they need.

While you're participating in the workshop, create a group on WhatsApp, Telegram, or a similar platform. Invite the colleagues who are participating in the workshop with you to join the group so you can discuss the course and ask and answer each other's questions. This way, even after the workshop, if you have questions or need advice, you have an established network of teachers at your fingertips.

Every time you attend a workshop, invite more teachers to join the group. I'm in contact with several chemistry teachers and we have good communication. When the syllabus for 2023 was released, I contacted one of the teachers to discuss the changes. We were able to discuss the differences quickly and easily through text messages.

How to sign up for the Pearson Edexcel Marking Workshop

For those of you who opt to teach the Pearson Edexcel curriculum, to follow is all the information you will need to sign up for one of their marking workshops.

I simply typed "How to sign up for the Pearson Edexcel Marking Workshop" into my search engine. The first search result that came up was "Live Training | Pearson qualifications." That's the one I clicked on, and I landed on the Pearson Qualifications home page.[6] All the links are in the reference section at the end of the book.

Pearson offers a variety of different training options, including:

1. Live training
2. On-demand and pre-recorded training

3. Self-guided training

Live Training

At the time of writing this book, Pearson Edexcel had not yet re-opened their live training sessions after the COVID-19 restrictions. However, you can visit their Live Training page on their website to confirm if they have since started in-person workshops in your area.[7]

In the meantime, here are the steps you would follow to register for any of the Pearson Edexcel training events:[8]

Step 1: Select the event you would like to attend. Both the in-person events and the online events are available to view on their calendar. You can filter the calendar by date, location, subject, qualification, or keyword. When you find the event you want to attend, click on the event title. This will allow you to view more details. Once you're sure this is the event you want to attend, click on the "Register" button.

Step 2: You will be asked to sign in or create an account. Once you have input all the necessary information, including your email, username, name, country, language, role, and password, you can click the "Submit" button.

Step 3: You will now make your way through the checkout pages. Once you have ticked that you agree to the terms and conditions, you can click on the "Finish" button. You will be asked to review and confirm your information.

Step 4: The last thing you need to do is simply provide payment information. You will receive a confirmation number and an email will be sent to you confirming the details of the event you have booked.

On-Demand and Pre-recorded Training

These on-demand training sessions can be viewed at a time that suits you. You can view them more than once, and they are available to share with colleagues.

Step 1: Select the qualification you want to view a training video on.

Step 2: Select a subject.

Step 3: A new page opens with all the information you need regarding upcoming courses on the subject and the level you chose.

Center-Based Training

Due to the COVID-19 restrictions, center-based training was being given as online center-based training at the time of writing this book. Center-based training would be a good idea if you can find a group of colleagues who want to do the same training so that you can split the cost between you.

How to sign up for the OxfordAQA Workshop

OxfordAQA offers several training webinars that you may be interested in should you choose to teach their curriculum.

The first one is the "Getting Started" webinar, which will provide you with all the information you need to tutor confidently. A subject expert will guide you through the specifications, the available resources, and the assessment approach. You will be given a detailed overview of the scope of work and the opportunity to ask questions.

To register for the Getting Started workshop, go to the OxfordAQA site,[9] click on Support, and then on Training Events. Under the Getting Started thumbnail, you will find and click on the "Register here" button.

A list of dates and corresponding sessions will open, with the option to "Register here" for the one you choose. I opted for Biology for the sake of this example.

The page that opened next gave me the name of the subject expert and the date and time that the webinar would take place. Times given are for the London time zone (GMT+1:00). You can select your time zone from the drop-down list so that you can see what time the webinar will happen where you are.

Next, you will fill in the details on the registration form, which include your name, email address, location, school or organization, center number, position, and an optional telephone number.

Read the privacy policy, tick the box, and then click on the "Register" button.

A confirmation page will open with the webinar details, including the URL you will need to join the webinar. You can join from a PC, Mac, iPad, iPhone, or Android device.

The other workshops you may want to join include:

1. Teacher Toolkit webinars
2. Prepare to Teach webinars
3. Go Further webinars
4. Pop-up training webinars

You will find all these webinars on the OxfordAQA site, under Support and then Training Events. Registration works the same as for the Getting Started webinar.

CHAPTER 3 IN A NUTSHELL

Your students need straight A+ grades. They're under a lot of pressure. Therefore, there is a demand for great teachers like you at every level and in every subject to equip them with everything they need to attain those outstanding results.

Past papers are a free tool that you can use in your teaching to add value to your student's learning process. You can also use them as a resource to grow your practice. They are freely available to download.

Enrolling in a marking workshop will set you up to be the kind of teacher your students need. You will get master the subject and learn how the exam boards want the questions answered. This kind of information is invaluable.

In Chapter 4, I will show you how to establish yourself as an expert and grow your online teaching practice without having to spend your money on advertising costs.

ESTABLISHING YOURSELF AS AN EXPERT

"Life isn't about trying to be an expert in everything. It's about being an expert in one thing and offering it to the world."

— *BO SANCHEZ*

We have been focusing inward until now—getting *you* ready to become an international online teacher. Now, it's time to focus outward.

This chapter is divided into two parts: building and reaching an audience, and then how to provide value for that audience. The thread that ties them together is the platforms that you will use to establish yourself as an expert teacher, communicate with students and parents, host your meetings and lessons, provide your resources, and grow your teaching practice.

PART 1: ENGAGING WITH PEOPLE ON SOCIAL MEDIA GROUPS

The need to build an audience

We're talking about tutoring international students, not learners from local high schools who already "know" you as a teacher.

We are aiming to tutor international students, specifically those from Middle Eastern countries, for a few reasons:

- They are taught in English, even though English may not be their first language.
- They are under huge pressure to attain the highest possible grades—an A+ in most of the eight subjects—or they may not be accepted into the university or college of their choice.
- Their parents are willing to pay an expert for additional teaching outside of their school

lessons because they understand the value in return for their investment.

You are not going to meet these parents in the hallway at school or at the grocery store. They don't know you exist. However, they are looking for someone with the skills that you possess. The only real barrier is letting them know you exist, that you are highly capable, and willing to teach their children.

To start with, my advice would be to join social media groups. You will find these groups on various platforms, including Facebook, WhatsApp, Telegram, or any other platform that is convenient and popular with students at the time of reading this book.

To follow is a bit more detail on each platform and how I used them to add value and grow my practice.

Groups on social media platforms

Facebook

If you have an existing Facebook profile, it will be relatively easy to find relevant groups to join. If you don't have an existing Facebook profile, I'd like to encourage you to create one, and when you do, be sure to include "Accounting Tutor" or "English Tutor" or whatever the case may be, to your profile.

For example, your Facebook name could be "Jessica Simmons—Physics Tutor."

Or you could include the words "English Tutor" in your Facebook bio. Your Facebook bio appears under your name on your home page and can be edited by clicking on the little pen icon. In the same vein, I'd like to encourage those with personal pages to add "Science Tutor" or "Math Tutor" to your profile name or bio.

You could create a new page altogether, like a business page, because you won't be relying on your current Facebook contacts to grow your international teaching practice. To create a new page, simply click on the menu icon at the top of your Facebook profile and select "Pages" from the drop-down menu. You can then click on the "+ Create New Page" button and follow the prompts.

Please note that at this stage, you are creating a "page" and not a "group." You might eventually create a Facebook group, but for now you just need a page that lets people know you are an online teacher.

Once you have your page ready, you can look for groups to join. Go to the home page on your profile and type corresponding keywords into the search pane. For example, I typed "Chemistry IGCSE Egypt," and the search results showed a public group called "IGCSE

Chemistry Questions and Answers" with over 12,000 members. You could join a similar group for the subject that you will be tutoring.

Be sure to read the group's rules and guidelines.

Once you're in the group, scroll through the posts and look for people who have shared links from other groups that you might be able to join. Also, look for shared links to WhatsApp or Telegram groups.

You will interact with people in these groups in two ways. Firstly, post hints, tips, and tricks that will help students in your subject. For example, as an English teacher, if you have a helpful way for students to remember when to use "there," "their," and "they're," this would be a great place to post it. If you are a math teacher and have a helpful way to remember the difference between acute and obtuse angles in geometry, share it. However, you can't just post once and be done; you need to post consistently and regularly. In a group with over 10,000 members, you need your posts to be visible and the only way to do that is to post regularly.

Be friendly and personable in your posts. Don't just add a link or infographic in the group. Say something like, "Hi everyone! I loved this and thought you might find it useful. Let me know what you think." Encourage engagement from others by asking open-ended questions that beg to be answered. From my experience, posts with eye-catching photos outperform posts that have no image.

The first thing I posted was a PDF document with questions and answers. Remember, in the previous chapter, I talked about past papers—this is what I meant when I said that you could use the documents you created to add free value to groups.

You can reuse the content you post, so do a good job creating it and save it all to a folder on your computer (or, better yet, a "cloud" drive like OneDrive, Google Drive, or Dropbox, for example, for added peace of mind that you will be able to access it in the future even if you get a new computer).

The first few months are a little more time-consuming because you are creating *new content* related to the IGCSE curriculum. However, every day new students and parents join the group who haven't seen any of the helpful guidance you previously posted. You can start reposting (reusing) *old content* after as little as a few months (depending on the content's relevance to the syllabus). Hooray! The bulk of the work is already done.

The second way you can interact in the groups is to respond to and answer other people's questions. Once again, be friendly and courteous. Introduce yourself as a teacher in the subject and then go on to answer the question. For example, "Hi Kate. That's a great question. I am a physics teacher and..." then go on to answer the question. As the subject teacher, you are best qualified to provide a thorough answer to all subject- and curriculum-related questions.

Dedicate a certain amount of time every day to answering students' questions, even if it's just half an hour. Commit to posting at least twice a week to get your name "out there," establish yourself as an expert in your subject, and add value to the group and its members.

After a while, you can create your own group and start inviting people to join. However, don't suddenly stop posting on the public groups. Most of your prospective students are in public groups, so you want to remain active until your private groups are well supported. You need quite a few people in your own group before you announce that you're starting online classes—it's all relative. When you start your own group, I recommend that you post all the content you shared on public groups. That way, your group will offer tremendous value to anyone who joins.

I felt that creating a group on WhatsApp was more impactful than Facebook. Although I've always used WhatsApp only with people I already know, when I started exploring online teaching, I found it to be used differently. Parents in many countries use WhatsApp private groups to support each other and provide helpful information about the IGCSE system. Teachers also create IGCSE-relevant groups as a marketing tool. That's exactly what I did: I created a group called "IGCSE Chemistry Help." I shared the group link in other IGCSE-relevant WhatsApp groups as well as on my Facebook page and Facebook group. The first thing I posted was my Chapter 1 question and answer document. Students then started asking questions, and I started answering them to the best of my ability. Sometimes I'd get questions from parents—for example, "My son wrote this, is it correct or not?"

I would respond by letting them know what he did right and what he did wrong. I would even go so far as telling them how many points he would have received if it had been a test question. The more personalized your answer, the more value it has, and the more that people will pay attention.

Once your group has gained momentum, your audience will guide you in what you should post about by telling you what they are struggling with. You will be able to pick this up from the questions that are being asked. You don't know what you don't know. When I started, I didn't know what people were struggling with; I let them tell me, and then I met them at the place where they needed me.

Create groups on any and every social media platform where your students and their parents hang out. Initially, it is a lot of work, but you will automatically ease off on the group posts once your tutoring practice is up and running.

Telegram and WhatsApp

Telegram and WhatsApp are free, multiplatform messaging apps that allow you to send text messages and voice messages, make voice and video calls, and share images, documents, and other content.

There are a few differences between them, mainly, the allowed number of members per group (currently Telegram allows larger groups). The best advantage of a Telegram group over WhatsApp is that all the content that was posted in the group will be available all the time, even to the newest members.

Based on the information above, you can decide which platform suits your needs, but remember that it's best to use the platforms your student and parents are most comfortable with. Platforms are culturally dependent, and new ones pop up from time to time, so stay up to date with what's trending. From my experience, students and parents from the Middle East mostly use

WhatsApp, Facebook, and Telegram. The IGCSE is a popular curriculum in the Middle East, thus they are an important target audience.

In the beginning, you may feel that you are spending a lot of time on the groups giving free value, but remember, you are investing time to establish yourself and confirm that you are good at explaining and answering questions. Once people get to know you and students sign up for your class, you will spend less time posting on the groups. Once you have established yourself as an expert, people will want to join your paid classes, and then others will join from word of mouth. Your happy parents and students will do free marketing for you.

PART 2: PROVIDING VALUE FOR THE STUDENTS

The importance of providing value to your audience

The parents you will be dealing with are very happy to invest in their child's education because they want them to get straight A's, get accepted to college, and get a degree. Your challenge will not be convincing the parents to pay for tuition; your challenge will be convincing them to pay *you* specifically. Why should they pay you over someone else? How will they know you are good enough? How will they know you are a great teacher who can help their child attain those results? You must prove yourself by providing free value for a little while. Once parents and students get to know you, like you, and understand you, you have potential students ready to enroll in your online class.

Ways you can provide free value

1. Post a short document. For example, post a question from a past exam paper and provide an A+ answer compared to a C answer. Explain and highlight what makes one answer worthy of an A+ grade.

2. Make a YouTube or TikTok video in which you explain an important concept or a common mistake. We will look at making videos in more detail in Chapter 6. Share the link to the video on the group with a brief explanation. You can share videos from other sources, provided they are informative and add value.

3. Encourage students to ask questions and praise those who ask by saying, "That's an excellent question, Amir."
Answer the questions as promptly as possible.
You can answer the question in various ways:
- Type up a detailed answer,

- Leave a detailed voice note,
- Or better yet, record yourself explaining on a whiteboard or a plain piece of paper and upload the video.

4. Another free service you can offer is to grade a student's paper and provide detailed feedback. This is by far the most valuable service. If you can provide them with a score and explain why they lost marks, they will follow you anywhere you go and hopefully enroll in your paid classes.

Don't post cold ads; they don't work. Cold ads are, for example, when you post something that says, "I'm a chemistry teacher, sign up with me."

Parents are immune to ads and respond to them negatively or simply ignore them. Parents want to hear from other parents. I've seen countless times on Facebook and WhatsApp where parents ask, "Who do you recommend for such-and-such subject? Please respond *based on your personal experience.*"

Once you've begun tutoring, you've proven yourself, and your students' grades have improved, you will see your name being mentioned in those recommendations, and then you'll know you've done it right.

Don't waste money on paid ads. I tried it; it didn't work. Parents are much more likely to trust word-of-mouth referrals when it comes to online teaching.

Additional insight for successful group management

People do realize that your free services can't last forever. If a teacher is good and has a paid course, parents know that this teacher will have to dedicate their time to the paying students rather than the free group. When you get to this stage consider posting one of your YouTube videos on your free value groups every few weeks; you don't want them to forget you.

The best time to establish yourself in groups and start your own groups is in the summer. Not only do you have a break from your everyday teaching, but your target students *haven't* taken a break—they are working through. This gives *you* the time you need to show off your skills, to demonstrate your dedication and passion.

Become acquainted with someone in the group, preferably one of the parents, who can help you translate any of the posts that are written in a foreign language. I have gotten to know several parents in my group—one of them has become a good friend who gives me invaluable cultural advice.

While you are providing free value, you may feel like you are spending a lot of time, but don't worry; this is only temporary. Once you have enough students in your class, you'll gradually reduce your free help.

Progressing from free groups to paid classes

Once people start to know you and like you, and begin engaging in the groups, you can announce that you will start providing online teaching. This announcement should contain specific information: what subject and level you will be teaching, the day and time of the sessions, your fees, how to sign up, and payment methods. We will cover more about payment methods in the next chapter; suffice to say, don't publish your bank information in a public group!

Before you announce your availability, make sure you determine the day and time of your class. It should be a time that works for *you* as well as for your students. Remember to consider the time difference and the fact that students must be in school during the day. Bear in mind that the weekend is on different days in Middle Eastern countries—namely Friday and Saturday. For me, Saturday worked perfectly because I don't have to go to my day job, and my students are off school that day too. I teach at 6 a.m. my time which is the afternoon for my students. For some it is 3 p.m.; for others, it's 4, 5, or 6 p.m., depending on their location. For me, this is perfect—it doesn't completely ruin my Saturdays, because I'm done by 8 a.m. and have the rest of my weekend to myself.

Other times that may work well for US-based teachers are early in the mornings on weekdays. It is harder to correlate, but it is possible. For example, on weekdays at 5 a.m. where you live, it may be late afternoon in other countries and your students will most likely be home from school. This means you can give your online class and be done before you start your day job.

If you get responses to your announcement that are not in English and you haven't yet found a friend to translate for you, Google Translate works like a charm.

To start, offer one free online class. This serves as an information session, or you could call it an orientation session. These information sessions and your online tutoring classes will take place on video conferencing software, such as Microsoft Teams, Google Hangouts, or Zoom.

Zoom is what I recommend. It allows two participants to be in a meeting for up to twenty-four hours. If you have between three and one hundred participants, you can host a meeting for up to forty minutes. However, neither of these options work if you need to host a meeting for any number of students for two hours; you will likely have to invest in an entry-level plan, which at the time of writing this book was just $14.99 per month. Zoom has also removed the forty-minute meeting limit on free accounts for K–12 educators.

During your information session, you will explain to prospective students how your class is structured. For example, during my first information session I told the students that the first half would be dedicated to discussing the common mistakes I saw in the home-work. The second half would be for explaining new material. I told them that they would have homework during the week that has to be submitted electronically, or they can take a picture and submit it on WhatsApp in time for me to mark it before the next session. Then, in the next class, I'll do the same thing—discuss the most common homework mistakes before I move on to new material.

I used the first half of my "information"—or "orienta-tion"—session to explain the structure of my class and my homework policy. I used the second half to start explaining Chapter 1. I pulled out all the skills I have as a good teacher: using students' names, encouraging them to ask questions, and answering their questions in a way that prompted them to answer their own ques-tions rather than *telling* them the answer outright.

At the end of the free session, I gave them my schedule and told them they could sign up on my website or contact me privately on WhatsApp so we can get started. When you give them your schedule, provide it in your time zone *and* their time zone too, to avoid any misunderstanding. Hopefully, after your orientation session somebody will sign up.

I started my class with just two students. But three more signed up within a few weeks, just from word of mouth; I didn't do any marketing. I didn't spend a penny on Facebook ads. In 2019, those five students studied with me for the whole academic year, and in 2020 I had twenty-five students sign up. I taught all twenty-five at once on Zoom on a Saturday morning, and I used WhatsApp during the week to support them.

The following year, I had more than one hundred students sign up, so I hired graders to assist me.

I know this sounds extremely simple, but in all honesty, my first orientation session was a failure. I was so nervous but super excited at the same time. I gave bad analogies and weak examples. The WebEx platform I was using at the time (a platform similar to Zoom) crashed halfway through. There were eight students. They were all very quiet and none of them had their video on. The session was fraught with newbie problems. After the session, parents thanked me and said that the kids were happy with the class, but no one signed up. I failed miserably. But because of my "nothing can stop me" mindset, I didn't give up. I knew I had great teaching skills and wanted to provide them to the students who needed them. I gave myself a couple of days to reset my mind and decided to host a second information session. Yes, I did it again. And the rest, as they say, is history!

Tips for a successful orientation session

I went through this failure and gained the required experience. I'm writing this book so you don't have to learn from your mistakes—learn from mine instead.

In the remainder of this section, I'm going to tell you exactly how to plan and run your first session, which is extremely important since it's the one that will determine if students enroll or not.

Again, use the first half of your information session to explain how you do things, and then use the second half to start teaching Chapter 1.

Here is a 4-step plan to ensure your first information session is a huge success:

1. Stay calm. You are a teacher; you teach every working day. Don't let nerves or excitement get the better of you. Have a script if you must—

but stick to the plan. Don't talk too much or too fast. Your students and their parents need to know that you are relatable. They need to understand you and "click" with you, so they sign up. Remember, though they are excellent English speakers, for most of them, English will be their second, if not third language!

2. Show your students (and their parents) your plan for the year. Having a schedule of when you cover certain chapters will prove to them that you won't just be teaching haphazardly. When they know that you take your job seriously enough to plan, they will trust you.

3. Set rules. Explain your homework policy— when it is due and how to submit it. Because my classes are on Saturdays, I ask my students to submit their homework by Thursday. If, for example, the homework is twenty-two pages, they will take a photo or scan each page and send it to me via WhatsApp privately (homework does not go on the group for obvious reasons). It's much easier if they submit the pages as one PDF file rather than twenty-two separate pictures of all twenty-two pages. But don't worry—your students are tech-savvy, they will know how to do this. Tell the students that if their homework is late, you will send one

WhatsApp reminder; after that, you will WhatsApp their parents. Their parents will appreciate that you are holding their children accountable for their homework and your students will be sure to complete it.

4. Start teaching Chapter 1 at an easy pace—not too slow and not too fast. Knowing whether you are too slow or too fast is a skill, but I'll explain how to determine their perception of your pace. At frequent intervals, ask one of the students to answer a simple yes/no question, then ask them *why*. Their answer will give you an idea of their current level. Then ask the rest of the group to tell you if they agree with the answer or not by simply typing "Yes" or "No" into the chat. Call on each student and give them an opportunity to answer an easy question. Yes, every single one. They all need to feel connected and will appreciate that you know and remember their names. Don't ask difficult or lengthy questions at this stage; that will frighten them away from your class. They are probably also feeling strange and uncomfortable. Answering an easy question will give them confidence and excitement about the upcoming lessons. You want them to leave

the class happy, proud of themselves, and looking forward to learning more.

Tips for successful online classes

This section of the book will confirm the basics of good teaching. You may know all of this already, especially if you are an experienced teacher. Still, I'd like to encourage you to read it and review your approach so that you can achieve the most successful teaching methods for your online teaching practice.

1. Embrace a positive mental attitude before each class

Make time to do things that recharge your energy. For me, this consists of things such as:

- Taking a warm bath or shower—the warm water helps you relax.
- Using an exfoliating scrub to help recharge the body by improving blood circulation.
- Drinking sufficient water.
- Eating high-fiber foods.
- Stretching and exercise.
- Walking outdoors (if you have a pet, this is a great excuse to get outside).
- Meditating.
- Getting enough sleep.

2. Be excited about each class

Every class offers you an opportunity to make a difference in the lives of your students. They may be feeling overwhelmed by all they have to do every day to achieve the best grades at the end of the year. Let your classes be a ray of light in their jam-packed week.

3. Plan before each class

You may be following a curriculum, but you can tailor each session to suit your individual teaching style and your learner's preferences, to offer them the best outcome. Spend some time familiarizing yourself with the teaching material so that the lessons flow smoothly and are fun for everyone.

4. Your lesson notes serve more than one purpose

Personalized notes with questions and answers can be sold to parents, students, or other teachers.

5. Lead your students to answer their own questions

When a student asks a question, don't just answer it—that doesn't teach them how to think or problem-solve. It is better to lead them to the answer. Less-experienced teachers answer the question straight up, as if to get the question out of the way. Instead, allow the question to become part of the lesson. A student who is led to answer their own question will more likely remember the answer than one who was just given it outright.

6. Create motivation and healthy competition among your students

Healthy competition occurs when it is not about the end result—of being the winner—but rather, about gaining other benefits, such as improving knowledge in a subject. Motivation and competitiveness among your students will encourage them to be eager for your lessons.

CHAPTER 4 IN A NUTSHELL

Getting your international teaching practice off the ground takes dedication, but after you have tilled the soil and planted the seeds, you will reap a harvest for many seasons to come.

Tilling the soil and planting the seeds are the hours you spend establishing yourself as an expert on public groups on social media. Soon you will be able to invite people to follow you to your own groups. This all takes place on Facebook, WhatsApp, Telegram, or whatever social media platform your target audience uses. The students you aim to teach don't necessarily live in your neighborhood or even your country, so conventional marketing methods won't work.

Reaping the harvest comes when you have students sign up for your live sessions. Based on my experience, the number of students in your lessons will grow exponentially year on year. Trust me; I've been there. I've made mistakes and learned the hard way the right and wrong way to do things. If you follow my guidelines, you could have a successful practice within a year, and you won't look back.

In Chapter 5, we will look at the two P's—parents and payments; they go together after all. I'll give you experiential advice on dealing with parents and practical advice on how to manage your payments, including detailed information about the different platforms through which you can receive payment.

Scan the QR code to watch this short training video called: The One Simple Secret.

COMMUNICATING WITH PARENTS AND ACCEPTING PAYMENTS

"Treat children as though they already are *the people they are capable of becoming.*"

— *HAIM GINOTT*

As a teacher, dealing with parents is par for the course. However, dealing with the parents of the students in your online teaching sessions won't be quite the same. For one thing, they are probably not from America, and their native language is probably not English. For another, they are willing to pay for additional tuition provided it helps their child achieve the grades they need to attend the college of their choice—

so they are likely to be very particular. The fact that you're running an international practice also makes receiving payment a little more complicated than accepting cash in an envelope from people in your hometown.

In this chapter, I will give you advice based on my own experience so that you don't have to "bang your head against a brick wall," as they say, trying to figure out how to do things.

Firstly, we'll look at dealing with parents. I'll give you examples of questions you can expect them to ask and what questions you should ask them in return. We'll discuss how to master communication and overcome negative issues, and I'll give you some insight on how to persuade them that you're the right teacher for their child.

Secondly, I'll give you practical advice on managing the administration of your live sessions and which platforms you can use to receive international payments.

PART 1: DEALING WITH PARENTS

What questions can you expect parents to ask?

When parents first contact you, they may have many questions. In my experience, these are the three most frequently asked questions:

Question 1: "How much do you charge?"

I don't want to put a dollar value on your sessions for several reasons.

Firstly, you may read this book years after I have written it, by which time my dollar value will be outdated. Secondly, how much you charge depends on several factors, including how qualified you are, how much teaching experience you have, and how much demand there is for tutorage in the subject and level you provide.

Another factor that could influence your rate is the number of students in your sessions. For instance, if your classes are small enough that each student is guaranteed personalized feedback on their homework, you can charge more per session than someone who teaches a lot of students and therefore can't provide that same level of individual attention.

When deciding what to charge, don't compare prices with American tutors, who are tutoring American students. But more importantly, don't be tempted to sell yourself short. You are a qualified professional offering a sought-after service. If some parents say you are too expensive, it doesn't mean you must drop your price. However, if every parent you speak to says your price is too high, you could possibly review your rate for the first year. Once your student's grades have improved and you have established yourself as an expert teacher, word-of-mouth referral will mean interest in your sessions is guaranteed; then, you can adjust your rates accordingly. The price I chose to offer is one that is on par with other online IGCSE teachers. In 2021, rates tend to fall between $16 and $25 per class, per student. Remember that your goal is to teach in groups, thus, your rate per hour will be multiplied by the number of students in your class.

Question 2: "How are payments made?"

You can receive international payments via PayPal, Payoneer, Stripe, or direct bank deposit. We will discuss these options in the next section of this chapter.

Question 3: "What is your system?"

When parents ask this question, what they really mean is, "What is your teaching approach?" They want to know the level of personalization you will give to their child and the level of accountability you expect from your students.

Please note—this is very important: The answer that will please them is that you correct their homework and provide feedback, that you hold the students accountable and make sure they are on the right track, and that you will inform the parents of their child's progress.

Parents will also ask other questions, so make sure you have answers ready. Here are some examples:

- What day and time do you have your sessions?
- On what platform do you host the sessions?
- What other subjects or levels do you teach?
- How much homework do you give?
- When must the homework be done by?
- How do students submit their homework?
- What is the maximum number of students you will allow in your classes?
- Do you only teach in English? Don't be nervous to answer yes to this question. The learners are being taught in English, so the parents *want* English-speaking teachers.

You would have answered these questions in your free information session, but not everyone who contacts you will have attended that session. If a new parent is referred to you by another, they will want to know everything. Equally, some might already have the information, but they will still want to hear it from you, personally.

Handy hint:

Type up a Q&A sheet with these questions and answers. Update it if you get asked any others. Even though you may have answered their questions in the call or the information session, forward the Q&A sheet—you could name it "frequently asked questions"—to each parent who contacts you. Not only will you look super organized, but they will be able to use the sheet to relay the information to their spouse or another parent. They will also have the document on record for future reference and it will help prevent any miscommunication.

What questions to ask the parents

Your goal as an international online teacher is to take a student from point A to point B—or, more aptly, from a B to an A! To do this most effectively, you need to know exactly where the student is currently at. The greater your understanding of their current level, strengths, and weaknesses, the better you will be able to help them move forward and level up.

You will learn these things from the students soon enough once you begin classes with them. Nevertheless, asking the parents ahead of time will enable you to start teaching proactively, resulting in the most benefit for the learner.

Plus, asking personalized questions about *their* child will prove to the parent that you have their best interests at heart. This is a great way to prove to parents that you are a great teacher.

Here are examples of some questions you can ask:

- What is your child's current level?
- What grades are they currently achieving?
- What areas are they struggling with?
- What do they need help with?
- Are they diligent at completing homework on time?

Handy hint:

Type up these questions—and any others you can think of—in a document. Once a parent has contacted you, forward these questions for them to complete, even before they commit to your class. Below, you will find the same list of questions rephrased to address the student and not the parent. The fact that you are interested enough to ask for this information now will impress the parents.

If the child completes the questionnaire but doesn't join your course, you don't need to spend time reviewing their answers; simply thank them for their responses and move on. However, if the learner does sign up for your course, you will have a wealth of information to aid you as you get started. Plus, you will have some handy documented evidence to base their progress on when you start giving feedback and doing evaluations.

Here are the rephrased questions that you can forward to the learner:

- What is your current level?
- What grades are you currently achieving?
- What areas are you struggling with?
- What do you need help with?
- Do you promise to complete homework on time?

Mastering communication and overcoming negative issues

Understandably, you may be nervous when new parents contact you. You may feel like you are being interviewed—and of course, in a way you are. Communication will likely be via WhatsApp (text, voice notes, or voice call) or similar.

Usually, these calls only take place at the beginning of the academic year. This is a good thing because it means you can quickly get on with the fun part of teaching and not have to worry about the interview stage for very long. However, it also means that you only have one chance to impress upon the parents that you are the best online teacher for their child.

Here are five tips to help you make the most of each call:

1. Give yourself time to prepare

Adopt a positive mental attitude. While we'd all love to be happy, joyful, and optimistic all the time, life happens, and we have some down moments. If you are tired, stressed, or "out of sorts" when a parent reaches out to you, don't feel pressured into taking the call immediately. Text back and provide a few different date and time options for them to choose from for a future call. It is perfectly acceptable for you not to be available 24/7. Allow yourself the opportunity to rest or refresh before jumping on any calls. After all, you only have one chance to make the best impression.

2. Plan what you want to say

To help you feel more comfortable, have the Q&A sheet with all the frequently asked questions and answers at hand for reference, so that your answers come easily and consistently.

3. Clarify until you understand

Take the time to understand the question being asked. Due to the language difference, you may need to clarify a point. It is better to be sure you understand the question rather than provide an unrelated answer.

4. Speak clearly

My sincere advice is don't talk too much—it makes you seem naïve, inexperienced, unprofessional, or desperate. Experienced teachers are succinct and to the point. You may have a lot of information to impart, and you want to make a good impression, but talking too fast and saying too much will only do the opposite. Speak slowly and clearly, avoid any colloquialisms—slang terms—and don't worry about asking the parent to repeat themselves if you don't quite understand what they are asking.

5. Ensure you won't be interrupted

Treat your parent interviews like business meetings because, in effect, that's what they are. The parents you are speaking to are interviewing you to establish if you are the right teacher for their child. When they choose you, they will become your clients—paying you for your services for an entire academic year. If your meeting is interrupted, they may find it unprofessional and assume that your online lessons will be interrupted too. If you can, try to have a neutral background when on camera or blur out your surroundings, and keep any pets or children out of view and out of earshot.

Stay optimistic

Don't let any negative comments allow you to become discouraged. Also, don't allow yourself to become offended or take anything personally. I've had my share of discouraging remarks, but I maintained a positive attitude and stayed optimistic. I knew I had what it took to be a great online teacher; I just needed to persuade the parents of that. Once I had students booked into my sessions, I let my teaching skills do the rest of the work in establishing me as a sought-after teacher.

Initially, the parents won't know you and this may lead them to sound skeptical. Don't become defensive if they ask a dozen questions about your qualifications. If you are young, they may doubt your experience. This was especially challenging for me at the beginning of my career. I started teaching in-person when I was twenty-two years old. Many parents didn't take me seriously—until they saw the results.

Rest assured, most of these negative issues will go away after you've had the time to prove yourself. When the parents who are referred to you call you, they already know who you are and how great you are at teaching. When that happens, you won't have to spend the entire call convincing them you're the right person to teach their child.

How to persuade parents that you're the right teacher for their child

In time, every parent in your network will know that you're a good teacher because your students' improved grades will speak volumes about your skill. When this happens, your calls with the parents will feel less like an interview and more like a conversation.

While you are still establishing yourself, you may need to work harder to convince parents to trust you, but that will come from being prepared for the call, planning what you want to say, and communicating clearly and professionally. Confidence in your own ability will help others have confidence in you too.

Here are a few things you can do to maximize your chances of success:

- Refer to the parents by name.
- If you know the name of their child, mention them by name, saying things like, "It would be a pleasure to teach Judy." Or "I noticed in the questionnaire that Omar said he struggles with XYZ."
- Bearing in mind that a few of your calls will take place on video such as on Zoom, make sure you look at the camera during the call (and not at yourself). Again, make sure to choose an uncluttered background in a well-lit room or blur your background, put your mobile phone on silent, and turn off notifications on your computer. Dress professionally and use engaging body language.
- Smile.
- Breathe.

PART 2: PRACTICAL ADVICE FOR MANAGING PAYMENTS

Administrative tasks can become a nightmare if you don't have a good system in place *before* you get busy. I would like to share a few tips and tricks with you before we move on to discuss the platforms through which you can receive international payments.

1. Charge parents for batches of sessions at a time, and not one by one. For example, I charge in batches of eight. Charging for each class individually, one by one, is a huge administrative workload; you do not want to have this extra burden on your time.

2. Keep a payment spreadsheet—you're likely to need this for tax purposes anyway. Write the student's name, the date you received payment, how many sessions they paid for, and the date that their paid sessions will end. Don't be afraid to send reminders: In the 7th week, for example, message or email the parent to remind them to renew their "subscription." Using a cool word like *subscription* and not "payment" or "fee" is a tactical move, so you don't seem like you are simply chasing money.

3. Keep a register and mark off when a child attends or is absent. This is for your records and to aid you with your feedback. If a child is absent, you can notify their parents. Whether you count the absenteeism as a lesson or add the missed lesson to the end of the eight weeks is at your discretion.

Here is an example of a table that serves as a record of payment, a register, and a reminder of when to email the parents about the next subscription.

R = Send reminder

F = Final lesson

X = Learner in attendance

A = Learner absent

Name	Date Paid	July 31	Aug 7	Aug 14	Aug 21	Aug 28	Sep 4	Sep 11	Sep 18	Sep 25	Oct 2
Abdul x 16	July 27	X	X	X	X	X	X				
Rami x 8	July 29	X	X	X	X	X	X	R	F		
Omar x 8	Aug 1		X	X	X	X	X		R	F	
Judy x 16	Aug 3		X	A	X	X	X				
Hana x 8	Aug 10			X	X	X	X			R	F

If a child is absent, you can give them access to recorded classes on your website. This is better than sending them the link to the zoom recording because the link can be shared with others. You don't want your online content to be available to others for free.

You will ask parents to pay for the eight sessions in advance. I have an option on my website that allows people to purchase a course that is titled "Buy eight sessions." Parents can use this option to purchase their sessions as my website "shop" is linked to a payment platform.

My website, IGCSEVideos.com, looks professional and people trust it. I will go into more detail about setting up a professional-looking website in Chapter 6. I also have recordings of my live classes available for purchase on my website, but more about that later.

Now, let's look at the different ways you can receive payment for your online teaching services.

If you are using a service such as QuickBooks or Fresh-Books for accounting and tax purposes already, you can invoice and take payments through these types of platforms, to make it that much easier. However, here are some of the more common options for accepting payments from parents:

PayPal

What is PayPal, and how does it work?

PayPal provides a quick and easy way to request and receive money online.[1] You can transfer and receive money internationally.

Anyone can send money to you; all they need is your email address, which would be linked to your PayPal account. You will receive an email notification whenever you receive payment. You can transfer the money to your bank account or use it to make a payment yourself.

You can open a PayPal account for free, but there are fees involved when you receive payments. The fees vary from country to country but are, at present, no more than 5 percent per transaction.

There are two types of PayPal accounts: Personal and Business. With a Personal account, you can make payments to and receive payments from almost anyone with an email address. Personal accounts, however, will display your name and email address and not a company name.

If you have created a business name for your online teaching practice, you can insert this name on your invoices if you wish.

I personally don't believe you need to open a Business PayPal account for your online teaching service because a Personal account should offer all you will need.

A step-by-step guide to opening your PayPal Account

Start by typing "How do I open a PayPal account" into your internet browser.

1. Go to the link and click "Sign up" for a PayPal account.
2. Select the type of account you would like to create and click "Get Started."
3. Enter the required information, which will include your first and last name, address, phone number, and email address, and click "Continue."
4. Follow the instructions to complete your account sign-up.
5. For your protection, you'll create a password for your account and select two security questions.

To receive international payments, you will need to verify your ID and address and link your bank account.

Follow these steps to link your bank account to your PayPal account:

- Go to your PayPal Wallet.
- Click "Link a bank." If you're using the app, click "Menu" and then "Banks and Cards."
- Search for your bank or select it from the list.

- Enter your online banking details to instantly link your bank account with your PayPal account.

It takes about three business days to transfer funds from your PayPal account to your bank account.

Stripe

What is Stripe, and how does it work?

Stripe is an online payment and credit card processing platform that allows for the safe and efficient processing of funds via credit card or bank transfer.[2] When you create an account, Stripe software will connect to the "shop" page on your website. If you're not planning on creating a website, you can simply send parents an email or linked invoice so they can pay online via a secure web page.

Signing up with Stripe is as easy as:

1. Click on "Sign up."
2. Verify the email address you used to sign up.
3. Activate your account.
4. Fill out your details.
5. Add your banking information.
6. Set up Stripe Connection.

7. Select the option "build a platform or marketplace."
8. Complete your Platform Profile.
9. Update your settings.
10. Check that Connect is enabled on your account and fill in your information.
11. Review your details and start charging parents!

You can open a Stripe Account for free, but there are transaction fees payable when you receive payments and apply for the funds to be transferred to your bank account. The fees vary from country to country but are usually no more than 5 percent per transaction.

Payoneer

What is Payoneer and how does it work?

Payoneer is another way you can receive international payments. Payoneer's fee structure has fees ranging between 1 and 3 percent. However, there are additional fees if you opt for a debit card.

Direct Bank Deposit

Some parents may want to pay the money directly into your bank account. It is perfectly safe to give your bank account details to parents in a private chat or email. You will have to provide them with your name, the name of your bank, the routing number, and the account number.

CHAPTER 5 IN A NUTSHELL

I started this chapter by giving you my experiential advice because I've literally "been there and done that." The guidance I'm giving you will help you make the most favorable impression on parents, so you don't waste time making "rookie" mistakes.

After reading this chapter, you will know what questions to expect and what questions you should ask. You will also have learned how to communicate with parents to your best advantage. Once you have persuaded parents that you are the right teacher for their children, you can go ahead and be the organized, awesome teacher who will help students improve their grades. Once that happens, your existing students and their parents will tell others about you, and your online teaching practice will blossom.

As such, you'll need a safe and reliable way to receive payment of fees, and this chapter provided several options for you to explore.

In the next chapter, we'll take a look at the "why" and "how" of building a professional-looking website to host your recorded classes, courses, pre-recorded videos, and written material like lesson notes and question and answer papers. It can also be a convenient way for parents to pay for your services.

Scan the QR code to watch this short training video called: The one important step to starting your practice.

YOU CAN CHANGE THE LIVES OF FELLOW TEACHERS!

Soon, your online teaching practice will be going well, and you'll have a full class of online students each academic year. You only need to spend a couple of hours each weekend to manage your online teaching practice. Your marketing largely takes care of itself now, mostly by word-of-mouth referral. Parents come to *you* now, asking for your help. Your day job is plodding along nicely.

But you'll likely remember the stress if those first few months, that first year, when you weren't sure what you were doing or if any of the hard work was going to pay off. You had this great book from that experienced author who shared her insights with you, and helped you become a success.

Unfortunately, lots of people don't have any guidance. They don't have a support network. They flounder and flop; their business sinks before it even starts.

Despite the desperate need for teachers in many parts of the world, there are still a great number of teachers who are struggling to find work where they live. Many teachers are single parents, predominantly single mothers, who may need the extra income but can't spare the time to take a second job, let alone afford a babysitter. For these people, the ability to teach students from home at a time of their choice may be a lifeline. It may be the thing that keeps them afloat, a way to generate an income, using their talents which, right now, are simply going to waste.

There is one way you can help.

It will cost you nothing, except for a minute of your time.

If you want to help spread the word, help struggling, overworked, and underpaid fellow teachers take control of their lives, seize the opportunity to make a second income doing what they love, and have a better quality of life, all you have to do is to **leave a review**.

If you are reading this on an e-reader or kindle, all you have to do is scroll to the bottom of the book, then swipe up and it will automatically prompt a review.

If you are listening to this on a platform such as audible, then all you have to do is hit the three dots on the top right of your device, click rate & review, then leave a few sentences about the book with a star rating.

If you a reading this on good old-fashioned paper, you can simply scan the QR code below or head on over to the book's page on Amazon or Goodreads and leave a review there.

Customer reviews

⭐⭐⭐⭐⭐ 4.8 out of 5

1,260 global ratings

5 star	████████	85%
4 star	█	11%
3 star	▌	3%
2 star		0%
1 star		1%

˅ How are ratings calculated?

Review this product

Share your thoughts with other customers

Write a customer review

If you know anyone you think would benefit from my guidance and advice, send them my way! Or better yet, send them a copy of my book — they'll thank you for it later.

Thank you for sticking with me through the first part of the book, now let's dive into some of the important tips that will grow your online teaching practice.

PS – "At the end of the day it's not about what you have or even what you've accomplished... it's about who you've lifted up, who you've made better. It's about what you've given back." – Denzel Washington

WHEN WOULD YOU NEED A WEBSITE?

"Organizing is what you do before you do something,

so that when you do it, it's not all mixed up."

— *A.A. MILNE*

DO YOU NEED A WEBSITE?

The most obvious reason businesses, private practitioners, doctors, lawyers, and almost every other kind of organization or practice need a website is to be "found" on the worldwide web. An online presence is the only way to be visible in an online search.

There is a chance that people will stumble upon your website during an online search, but that is not the primary reason why I'm encouraging you to create a website for your online teaching practice.

You will reach most of your students and their parents through social media groups. The reason you need a website is to have an organized, professional-looking place to store your teaching material that is easily accessible to your students. A website can also provide an onsite payment facility, to give parents a convenient way to pay for your services.

As a teacher, you are going to have several resources on hand that you will want to provide free to your students but sell to others. A website is a great place to host your recorded Zoom lessons, pre-recorded videos, lesson plans, question and answer sheets, and all the other resources that you have created for your sessions.

Your website can be built using a learning management system (LMS) like Thinkific, Teachable, or Kajabi, rather than a regular website platform like WordPress or Squarespace. The reason is that an LMS will provide all the tools and features you need for your teaching practice without having to hire a web expert to build a website for you from scratch.

It is possible to run an online teaching practice without a website. You could use WhatsApp or Telegram to communicate with your students outside of live Zoom classes, and email documents and links to them as needed. However, this is very time-consuming and will cause limitations—your practice won't be able to grow to the proportions I'm advocating in this book.

WHICH LEARNING MANAGEMENT SYSTEM IS BEST FOR YOU?

Picking the right learning management system can make a huge difference to your overall online experience. There are many factors to consider apart from the obvious things like the cost and features.

Before I jump into comparing these three systems, I want to remind you that the *quality* of the content you offer on your platform is much more important than *where* you host it.

Let's compare Thinkific, Teachable, and Kajabi

1. Pricing
Kajabi is the most expensive, but it provides many more features than Thinkific and Teachable, which are equal contenders.[1]

Kajabi's entry-level plan offers more than the other two, and all three platforms offer tiered pricing.

Please note that prices are valid at the time of writing this book and that discounts are offered if you pay for the year in advance.

Here is a breakdown of their pricing:

Price per month	Kajabi	Thinkific	Teachable
Free	None	Yes—with a limit of 3 courses	Yes—with limited features
Tier 1	$149	$49	$29
Tier 2	$199	$99	$99
Tier 3	$399	$499	$249

As the prices go up, you get access to more features.

Kajabi looks to be the most expensive at first glance, but if you dig a little deeper, you will see that it is because Kajabi includes things like an email service, a blog hosting platform, webinar space, and similar tools. If you opt for Thinkific or Teachable, you have to pay for add-ons separately, depending on what you aim to achieve with your learning management system.

If you're going full-out from the get-go, it may be worth your while to get everything from Kajabi in one go. If you want to grow your system slowly, opt for an entry-level system; you can always upgrade and expand when you need to.

2. Payment and integration fees

All three of these system platforms offer 0 percent transaction fees but require that you partner with a payment gateway like PayPal or Stripe. Refer to the details about these and other payment systems at the end of Chapter 5. Please note, the Tier 1 Teachable plan incurs an additional 5 percent transaction fee over and above the gateway transaction fee, which, for Stripe, is 2.9 percent plus $0.30 for every transaction, at the time of writing. The cheapest plan is not necessarily the best —all features need to be considered.

3. Course design and student interface

All three platforms have a design interface that most people will be happy to use.

Here are a few key points regarding some of the features offered on each platform:

- Kajabi offers elements for text, video, and audio all on one page. To achieve the same effect on Teachable, you would have to embed the video or audio player in a text block.
- The course progress indicators on Kajabi are not as noticeable as on Thinkific or Teachable.
- The sidebar on Teachable may be a little busy compared to the other two, but all three sites look professional.

4. Teacher features

Teacher features include all the tools you will need to help you navigate the platform and see your students succeed on a consistent basis. These features include tracking each student's progress, seeing which items are the most popular, and seeing which are performing better than others.

All three platforms offer the ability to test your learners with quizzes and collect feedback using surveys.

5. Revenue reporting

Each of the platforms offers tools so you can see how much money you're making and where it's coming from. In the beginning, you won't need lots of detailed analytics with revenue projections and calculations, but it's good to know that, as your practice grows, your platform can grow with you.

More about Thinkific.com

My personal recommendation is Thinkific.[2] It offers everything you need. It is user-friendly and can certainly be used to build a professional-looking site that is easy for you and your students to navigate. Additionally, you can use Thinkific for free if you have a simple teaching program, which is probably the case for most teachers.

Here is a list of Thinkific's features:

- It is the only course platform with a free option and no additional transaction fees.
- Thinkific is the only platform to offer telephone support.
- It is easy to customize—you can tailor the platform to match the theme of your practice.
- Thinkific comes with a voice-over PowerPoint presentation tool making video production easy.
- It offers payment plans—like a monthly payback option for more expensive courses.
- It offers a monthly recurring subscription for ongoing enrollment in a course.
- It ties into 3rd party email providers like MailChimp for email marketing.
- It ties into 3rd party sales funnel builders like ClickFunnels.

Thinkific's free plan really is one of a kind

Thinkific is the only course platform that offers a worthwhile, long-term, free option. Other course providers have two-week free trials, or their free plans require you to pay transaction fees.

Thinkific's free plan has no hidden fees and offers all the features you need right now. You can set up a course, run quizzes, tailor your branding, and collect payments. If you need more features later, you can upgrade to one of Thinkific's paid plans.

Thinkific offers more customization options than any other platform. You can add branding to your courses, surveys, discussions, prerequisite lessons, completion certificates, and more. Plus, all the features are user-friendly.

WHAT TO PUT ON YOUR WEBSITE?

I would recommend that you have a four-page website: About us, Products, Links to social media accounts, and Reviews. Your landing page will also have a "Sign up" or "Log in" button.

1. About us
The "About us" section of your website is where you will introduce yourself to people. Here you will include your mission, vision, and values as well as some information about your qualifications and experience.

2. Products: All your teaching resources
This page is where you will put your courses, question and answer papers, lesson plans, pre-recorded classes,

recordings of your Zoom sessions, past papers, links to free value items, and all other tutoring resources. You can choose if your course will be shown on the homepage or "hidden." Anyone who visits your site will see all the courses that you don't hide. "Hidden" courses are for your enrolled students only. You will provide course access to the students who are part of your paid course.

Let's take a look at these "products" in more detail:

Question and answer papers

In Chapter 1, I introduced the idea of scouring past exam papers and creating question and answer sheets relevant to each chapter of the syllabus. You could have a tab on your website for these papers; they will be freely available to logged-in users, or available for purchase by anyone who has not enrolled in your program.

i. Lesson plans

Parents and other teachers may want to purchase your lesson plans, so be sure to include a tab for them on your products page, too.

ii. Pre-recorded classes

You can make pre-recorded classes available to your enrolled students as well as for sale to students who have not enrolled. Pre-recorded lessons can be filmed in several ways: Firstly, you can make a screen recording of your computer while you teach. Secondly, you can make a recording of your hands while you teach a lesson on paper or a whiteboard. Double-check to make sure everything you do is visible after you have made the video. Finally, you can record yourself speaking into the camera while you are seated at a desk or standing in front of a whiteboard. You may feel nervous initially and have to shoot and re-shoot the videos until you think they are good enough. You will get better with practice—I promise.

Pre-recorded classes and recordings of your zoom sessions are a great resource that you can sell on your website. I have also recorded my chemistry course offline (i.e., without students) and offer these videos in a course for sale. Students can watch these videos any time and do not have to follow my live class schedule.

Do I need special equipment to make a video?

- You don't need expensive equipment to make a video. You can use the webcam on your laptop or PC, the camera on your smartphone, or free screen-recording software.
- If you're sitting or standing still while filming,

you may get away with balancing your phone or camera on a stack of books, but camera stands and tripods aren't expensive.

- Natural light is the best light to film in. You don't need fancy lighting, but you do need *good* lighting.

- Poor audio quality will ruin even the best videos. The best way to guarantee good audio quality is to use an external microphone rather than the one built into your camera or mobile phone.

- If you need to edit your video, you can use free video editing software like Lightworks, VideoPad, or HitFilm Express. If you're using a Mac, it comes with free video editing software called iMovie. If you're nervous about video editing and have never done it before, there are lots of online tutorials on how to use this software on websites such as YouTube, for example.

Tips for creating the best videos without having to hire a production crew:

- Close unnecessary windows and tabs before you start a screen recording.

- Test your microphone volume; make sure it has the best quality.
- Make the recording in a quiet environment where there is no chance of interruption or distraction.
- Put your phone on silent and turn off device notifications to avoid interruptions.
- Whether you're nervous or familiar with your video content, don't be tempted to rush through the lesson too quickly.
- It doesn't matter how well you know your subject matter, make notes before you hit record. There is a chance you will get distracted, or nervousness can make your brain freeze.

iii. Recordings of your Zoom sessions

These are screen recordings of the actual live sessions that you provide to your students. They are especially useful for students who missed a class, but they are also a great resource tool on your website. You can sell these individually or in bundles.

The students who have enrolled in your online tutorship program will benefit from watching your classes more than once, and those who missed a class will need to watch the recording to catch up. To allow your students to watch the recordings, you will give them the login details to access that part of your website. Students who have not enrolled in your tutorship program will have the option to purchase your recordings through your website.

Zoom has a feature that allows you to record your Zoom sessions. After the live session is over, the recording is available for download from Zoom's cloud (MS Teams also has the same feature if you prefer this platform). This feature is terrific because it means you don't have the hassle of additional screen-recording software.

How Zoom helps teachers and tutors
There are many other platforms available that have similar features, but personally, I prefer Zoom. Teachers don't need the paid version of Zoom; the free version provides all the features you'll ever need, including hosting meetings with up to one hundred participants. Zoom also allows students to wordlessly indicate that they have a question, brainstorm on a virtual whiteboard, and collaborate on projects.

iv. Past papers

Past papers are available online for free, but you can include them on your website for added value.

v. Free value items

One thing that increased my student enrollment was my free value items. I've had many students say, "I joined because I watched your free video. It helped me not only understand the concept, but I also enjoyed the video and started to like chemistry!"

This point illustrates the value of providing free content and encourages you to make sure all your content is of the best quality. The assumption will be that if your free stuff is of good quality, then your paid classes will be excellent. On the flip side, if your free stuff isn't great, you won't attract anyone to your paid classes.

Having all your products on your website makes it very easy for parents to purchase things from you, because your website "shop" is connected to a payment gateway, such as PayPal or Stripe. This is why I have my classes in batches of eight available for purchase on my website

—there is much less admin involved if I sell them this way.

3. Links to social media accounts

Incorporate a link to your Facebook page, for example, so that people can go there straight from your website. And while I'm on this subject, make sure your Facebook page has a link back to your website, too. Also, if you have uploaded your pre-recorded videos or recordings of live sessions onto YouTube, be sure to create a link to YouTube from your website as well. And, again, make sure your YouTube page has a link in the description that directs people back to your website. They should all be connected to one another.

4. Reviews

The one thing that is going to make your practice grow exponentially is reviews. Once your students' grades start improving and they tell their friends how your lessons have helped them improve their grades, you will have students queueing to join your online classes. Once your students start doing well, they will send you messages telling you about their improved grades and thanking you for being such a great teacher. Share these messages and any other positive reviews you get on your website so that people who visit your site have third-party evidence that you are a great teacher. I take screenshots of the messages students and their parents send me, thanking me for my classes and telling me about their improved results. I share these screenshots on the review page of my website and on Facebook.

Hosting guest content on your website

You can invite other teachers to share samples of their products with you and host them on your website. This service will benefit you and other teachers in multiple ways. Your website will offer visitors more variety and greater value. Different teachers will gain exposure through you sharing their content. And other teachers may return the favor, allowing you to gain exposure from their website traffic in return.

CHAPTER 6 IN A NUTSHELL

Although your website will gain online exposure for your practice, the main reason you need a professional-looking website is so that you have a place to showcase all your resources, from exam papers to videos and anything in between. It also makes parents feel more secure that you are a serious professional and they won't be wasting their time or money by hiring you.

If you were nervous about making videos, I trust that the information I shared in this chapter helps you feel more confident about creating this valuable resource.

A website allows you to have some resources available for free, others open to those with log-in details, and others for sale to anyone that hasn't enrolled in your classes. The fact that your website is linked to a payment gateway will make your life so much easier!

Creating a website on a learning management system such as Thinkific, Teachable, or Kajabi is not difficult. I did it without the help of a website developer. The sites are specifically designed for teachers and tutors like you and me.

In the next chapter, we will fast-forward to a time when your hard work has paid off, and your teaching practice is bursting at the seams because your happy parents and students have referred you to others who want to enroll in your course. At this stage, you will need to work smart and outsource some of your tasks.

SECRETS TO SCALING YOUR PRACTICE

"Work hard, and you will earn good rewards. Work smart, and you will earn great rewards. Work hard and work smart, and you will earn extraordinary rewards."

— *MATSHONA DHLIWAYO*

GROWING YOUR TEACHING PRACTICE

A great deal of research goes into marketing. It's a billion-dollar industry. Marketing studies have found that word-of-mouth advertising is more effective than any other kind.[1] Why? Because people trust what other people say—especially if they can back it up with evidence. The evidence, in this case, is an improvement in your students' grades. When results are released, parents circle the social media platforms to see whose grades have improved or who got an A+, and then they want to know who that student studied with so they can call that teacher for their own children.

Let word-of-mouth do the advertising work for you

You may be tempted to spend money on Facebook or Google ads. I did. But in hindsight, my practice went from two students to more than one hundred because of word of mouth, not because of any advertisements I paid for. I used Google ads to sell notes and pre-recorded videos. I also used Google ads to bring traffic to my website, but only for a short time; once I had a few thousand students following me, I stopped paying for ads and allowed my site to grow organically.

Once my enrolled students' grades started to improve, and once I had proven to be a good teacher that my learners could understand and enjoy, they talked to their friends. Their friends then enrolled in my classes. This is word-of-mouth marketing at its best.

Facebook and Google ads did not help my practice grow. Doing a great job, helping my students, giving feedback to parents, and being attentive to those enrolled in my course are what made people happy. And happy people tell other people.

All you have to do is be an awesome teacher, and students and their parents will do all your marketing for you—for free!

Using your website to grow your practice

Your practice will also grow when students visit your website and see details about your course. Parents and students will find your website if you post links to it on your Facebook page and in your WhatsApp or Telegram groups.

Your website, social media pages, and messaging platform work together like the legs of a tripod—they link to each other. People who visit one can be easily directed to the others; that way, your platforms market one another, which is another type of free marketing.

I host my materials on a website so students can access them anytime. Plus, it saves me time because I don't have to email the students whenever they want my materials. Once they join, I give them access to my course so they can view, download, and watch everything anytime they choose.

Using other websites to grow your practice

Other existing websites offer to connect teachers with students. The site will feature your services, students or parents will find *you*, and the website will take a percentage of your fee. It's like an employment agency or a freelance marketplace, but for teachers and tutors. Some of the websites that you may be familiar with that offer this service are Outschool.com, Care.com, and FirstTutors.com.

Outschool.com explains that the benefits of teaching with them are as follows:

- Earn money flexibly. Teach online from your home and on your schedule.
- Be creative. Design your curriculum and teach the way you want.
- Motivated learners. Work with learners who have chosen to be in your class.
- No bureaucracy. Spend your time on teaching, not paperwork.

The downside is that on Outschool.com and Care.com, among similar websites, you will be one of many teachers providing online classes to students. These sites are very broad in the choices they offer. Parents visiting those websites are looking for a wide variety of needs. The likelihood of visiting parents needing your specific service is slim. Therefore, you want to be featured on an IGCSE-specific website (or whatever qualification and level you are teaching). Websites dedicated to IGCSE will be more beneficial because parents visit the website specifically looking for IGCSE teachers. There aren't many, which increases the likelihood of parents finding you.

Here are the top three websites that are IGCSE specific:

- IGCSEVideos.com
- Eshra7ly.com
- Mozakrah.com

In their "About" section, Eshra7ly confirms something I have been telling you all along:

"Because we know that IGCSE students in Gulf countries struggle to find good teachers with reasonable prices, we came to save the day!"

Do you see that? Students are struggling to find teachers who can tutor the IGCSE curriculum. I hope this confirmation encourages you to pursue this avenue and start your own online teaching practice.

Eshra7ly.com currently has thirty teachers offering eighty courses to 5,000 students. Did you notice the demand versus supply? There are 5,000 students, but only thirty teachers! I hope you appreciate how these numbers confirm the shortage of IGCSE teachers, specifically. I believe this review from a student who used Eshra7ly will also encourage you:

"Eshra7ly.com helped me a lot with my examinations. I got the score I needed to join the university of my dreams!"

Joining someone else's website is great because you get exposure to thousands of students and parents, but these sites take a percentage of your fees—about 35 percent at the time of writing. However, it can be worth it because you get greater exposure to potential students.

In the beginning, things will be slow because people don't know you. But that's okay because by using all the tips and tricks provided you can market yourself, grow your exposure, and make sure people find you.

If you need additional training on gaining exposure, you can get training at teachinternationally.online/onlineteaching. You don't have to spend time trying to figure out how to market your teaching practice to your best advantage—I did all the groundwork already, so let me help you!

Using an email list to grow your practice

An email list is another way to grow your practice. There are several email marketing platforms that offer free plans, such as MailChimp, ActiveCampaign, Moosend, and HubSpot to name just a few. However, free plans usually have some limitations—mostly to do with the number of emails that can be sent per day or per month. You can start with a free plan and upgrade as your email list grows. Once you have the email list, you can use an emailing platform like MailChimp to send the email to thousands of people at a time.

Collecting addresses is the most time-consuming part. To grow my email list, I offered a free download of a chemistry document. I paid for Google ads to promote the document. The download form requested an email address. In other words, a free gift in exchange for a name and email address. It took a long time and a great deal of marketing, but eventually I gathered a list of 2,500 students' emails. However, you don't have to build an email list to start your online teaching practice. This is just another option, and something I did myself. If you like the sound of this, I suggest you follow my strategy in Chapter 4 and be sure to get my training at teachinternationally.online/onlineteaching.

WORK SMART BY OUTSOURCING

At the risk of sounding like Dr. Seuss: There is only one you, that is truer than true. So, when it comes to growing your online teaching practice, being a full-time teacher, and having a life, *one you* can only do so much. Cloning isn't an option. What else can you do? For your teaching practice to grow, you will have to outsource many tasks.

Have you heard of the concept of multiplying your time? And I don't mean wishing for a thirty-six-hour day because then you will just be even busier than you already are.

Multiplying your time has more to do with using your time wisely today to buy yourself more time tomorrow. A practical example of this is automating your bill payments. It may take a couple of hours in one go, but once it's done you will save an hour a month on bill payments. A lot of the tips I've given you throughout this book are time multipliers (also known as time-savers).

Here are a few examples of some of the time multipliers I've shared with you:

- Create and save great Facebook posts that you can use again at the same time next year.

- Go through past papers and draw up question and answer sheets that will become a great resource in your practice. You can give them to your new students year after year.
- Create a website to help you store everything so that it's easily accessible to everyone rather than having to keep on emailing things to people.
- A website that is linked to a payment gateway will also help you manage payments.

Although they take time now, all these examples are time multipliers because they will save you time in the future.

Another way that you can multiply your time is by delegating or teaching someone else to do something as if you were doing it yourself. In other words, outsourcing. It may take a bit of time to find the right person and train them up, but in effect, you are creating another "you" to share the load with.

Eventually, when your practice grows, you will end up outsourcing everything except teaching. Ideally, you want to get to the place where the only thing you need to do is click on that Zoom link and teach.

You will be able to outsource scheduling, collecting payments, and even grading. To be able to outsource effectively and efficiently in the future, you need to do all these things yourself for a year or two. You need to understand everything about these tasks before you can train someone else to do them on your behalf.

Perhaps you feel that employing someone to do some of these tasks is shirking your responsibility, but I want to assure you that it is completely above board. In fact, by outsourcing administrative tasks and grading, you're freeing up extra energy to invest in teaching, which is, after all, the thing you love doing the most and what students' parents are paying you for. Unfortunately, admin is par for the course and cannot be ignored, but rather than allowing your admin duties to tie you down and restrict your growth, pay someone else to do it for you and enjoy the extra time this buys you to focus on the important things.

Parents don't care who schedules your classes or reconciles payments; they care about the facetime their child gets with you and the energy you have during your classes. The most important thing is that you teach in a way that your students enjoy and understand, that you follow up and make them accountable—make sure they do their homework, test them frequently, assess them—and then provide feedback to their parents.

When you get to the place where you have twenty-five or more students, doing everything yourself will be very time-consuming. You have worked hard to get here; now it's time to work smart.

What tasks can you outsource?

Let's take a look at the tasks you can outsource, where you can find the right people, and how to train and manage them most effectively.

Administrative assistant

One of the first jobs you can outsource is admin. This will include scheduling your live classes, reconciling payments and sending payment reminders, uploading new courses to your website, correspondence, and managing your social media accounts. One person can perform all these tasks, and because of the wonders of modern technology, this person can live in any country. After all, you are tutoring international students! The term for this type of work is "virtual assistant." A virtual assistant is generally self-employed and provides professional administrative, technical, or creative assistance to clients remotely from a home office.

Where to find an administrative assistant:

The best way to find an assistant is to ask for referrals. People who come with a recommendation are more likely to perform well. You can ask on LinkedIn as well as other social media groups. Potential employees may reach out to you through one of your groups or after seeing your post on social media.

You will also be able to find a virtual assistant online. Websites such as OnlineJobs.ph, Upwork.com, Fiverr.com, and Zapier.com have many virtual assistants looking for part-time or full-time work.

Whether they reach out to you, or you find them through an agency, you should interview all candidates to ensure you find the person best suited for the tasks you need to be done. Apart from fitting the job description, you and your prospective assistant need to "click"—you will need them to think like you do, or at least understand your goals.

What to look for in an administrative assistant:

- Availability. Bear in mind any differences in time zones if you want someone who is available at the touch of a button.
- Communication skills. If your assistant is handling your communications for you, it's best if they are good at English and can communicate clearly.
- Good organizational skills. They will be handling a whole bunch of tasks for you every day; some things are time-sensitive and others require accuracy. You can't have someone

irresponsible in charge of such important matters.

- Teachability. You need someone willing to learn tasks that are specific to your teaching practice and your way of doing things.
- Good work ethic. You're going to invest a fair amount of time training someone; it will be good to know they will stick around to make the investment worthwhile.

How to train an administrative assistant:

The best way to train an assistant is through a hands-on approach. This doesn't mean you have to be in the same room, though. Online video conferencing platforms such as Zoom, along with screen sharing, make remote training possible. During your Zoom calls, you will show your assistant what you need them to do. You could provide them with screen recordings of some of the more complicated processes so they can learn and practice until they are familiar with the tasks. As they become more proficient, they will be able to do things more efficiently and you can give them more responsibility.

How to manage an administrative assistant:

Human beings make mistakes and life happens, so keep in touch with your assistant so there is always an open channel of communication. Be gracious but hold them accountable. The success of your practice depends firstly on the solid foundation that you've already put in place, and secondly, on continued growth and development in two areas: teaching and administration.

To help you effectively manage your assistant, you can make use of free time-tracking software that takes screenshots. Examples of time-tracking software are TopTracker, TimeCamp, and Hubstaff, but there are many others. If you find your virtual assistant through Upwork.com, they can track their time through their platform and it will automatically track their working hours and use screenshots, and then pay them accordingly at the end of the week so you don't have to worry about it. I prefer offering a monthly salary, so I don't have to worry about tracking hours, but it is a personal choice.

Grading assistant

As a busy teacher, you already have a load of grading on your hands. You'd have to be super-human to grade twenty-five or more students' homework and assessments. This is where you need a grading assistant.

Where to find a grading assistant:

I found a grading assistant by letting my students know that I was open to hiring. One of my past student's older siblings reached out to me, saying he was interested in the job. He is doing wonderfully, most likely because he is familiar with my teaching approach. You could hire an IGCSE teacher to do your grading for you, as they are familiar with the curriculum and exams making them perfect for the job. You could also find grading assistants by asking for referrals, advertising on social media, or hiring online through websites such as indeed.com or Upwork.com.

Whether they reach out to you, or you find them through an agency, you should interview all candidates. You will be working together closely; you need to get on well.

What to look for in a grading assistant:

A grading assistant is responsible for the grading of homework, quizzes, and exams. Graders are expected to know all background and teaching material necessary for accurate grading. However, you will be providing them with the ideal answers to make their work as accurate as possible.

Apart from this, you need a grading assistant who is:

- Available to grade at the times you need them.
- Able to return the graded work within twenty-

four hours. Quick feedback is helpful to your students.

- Organized and can keep concise records of students, their grades, and associated comments.
- Teachable, so they grade in a way that aligns with your methods.
- Reliable, honest, and trustworthy.

How to train a grading assistant:

The best option would be to have someone who has attended one of the grading workshops we spoke about in Chapter 3. Your grading doesn't have to be done by someone in the US; you could look for an assistant in any country.

How to manage a grading assistant:

Make sure they are aware of your schedule and comply with your deadlines. You can negotiate a rate per hour or a rate per assignment, quiz, or exam. Like paying an administrator, I prefer offering a monthly salary, so I don't have to worry about tracking hours or the number of assignments graded. One more important tip: make your expectations very clear before hiring your assistant. For example, the expected workload, expected hours per week, and whether you expect them to answer questions when students post a question on the WhatsApp group, for example. It will be easier to manage a grading assistant than an administrative assistant because their progress will be immediate and obvious as you receive the graded papers.

First and foremost, it's your teaching practice

It can be so easy to get caught up in all the jobs we have to do that we lose sight of the "why" behind it all, as discussed in Chapter 1.

For your practice to be successful and provide the most value to your students, make sure they are being supported. Once you have a team of people helping you, you can have someone available to help students almost 24/7. No matter what time zone they are in, there will always be someone they can reach out to.

CHAPTER 7 IN A NUTSHELL

I'm encouraging you to grow your teaching practice. That growth can take place from word-of-mouth marketing, organically online, with paid marketing, or with a little help from your friends, i.e., me.

Word-of-mouth marketing is the best way to get students to enroll in your online classes. Do your job well, and parents and students will become your best marketing agents. Organic growth will happen if you use your website, social media groups, and messaging platforms to promote each other. Organic growth is slow but steady and has a snowball effect—it picks up speed the bigger it gets. Paid marketing can get very expensive and doesn't always work because of the way platforms change their algorithms.

What I have offered you throughout this book is the opportunity to grow your teaching practice. Learn from my experience and mistakes and you can jump straight in the deep end and swim. There's enough information in this book to help you successfully start and grow your own online teaching practice. However, if you would like more information, you can get training at the following web address: teachinternationally.online/onlineteaching.

The growth in your tutoring practice will put extra pressure on your time. You are just one person with twenty-four hours in a day like everyone else. When things get busy, you will benefit from time-multiplying practices like uploading your resources to a website. You will also benefit from outsourcing administrative tasks and grading. You will be able to hire virtual assistants and grading assistants from online agencies, and time tracking software will make managing them very easy.

As we end the last chapter of this book, I want to remind you one more time: You have skills that dozens of international students are looking for. With an investment of time and dedication, you can have a successful teaching practice up and running within one year if you allow the lessons I learned to guide you in how to do it properly.

Please read the conclusion. It sums up the book concisely, reminding you of everything you have already learned and offering a quick point of reference should you want to go back and review some of the information for deeper insight.

CONCLUSION: THE BOOK IN A NUTSHELL

We have reached the end of the book, but I'd like to remind you of the beginning: Where it all started for me.

In 2019, I started a "Chemistry Help" group on WhatsApp and invited students and parents from other groups to join. I announced that I would provide free help and materials. I started posting free chemistry PDFs and encouraged students to ask questions. I then answered their questions using WhatsApp's voice note feature. I was as generous and helpful as possible. I really wanted to show off my skills as a teacher.

At the beginning of the new academic year, I announced on this free group that I would host a live class every Saturday and invited everyone who was interested to attend a free orientation session, after which two students signed up. A few months later, three more students signed up. One year later, at the start of the 2020 academic year, I had twenty-five students sign up for my class. I now teach more than one hundred students.

When you provide superb services and your students feel supported, you will be unstoppable.

My students are from Egypt, Saudi Arabia, the United Arab Emirates, Kuwait, Qatar, Oman, Turkey, Tunisia, and Singapore. They go to private international schools and are taught the British IGCSE curriculum. Because they have to get A+s and As in almost all subjects to be accepted into the university of their choice, they need English-speaking teachers who are familiar with the IGSCE curriculum to teach them. The fact that you are a native speaker is a plus for you. Many students commented on my "good" accent, saying that some teachers have heavy English accents that they cannot understand.

My students and thousands of others from these countries are on WhatsApp, Telegram, and Facebook, looking for someone to help them get good grades.

I was born and raised in the UAE before moving to the States in 2007, so I am familiar with the international culture. The new generation of students in these countries is very well educated in international schools where the language of tuition is English. Their teachers are a bit older and were not educated in international schools. It will take years for the newer generation of teachers to fill this huge gap. Cue you and your teaching skills!

Thanks to this book, you are now fully equipped to start your own online international teaching practice.

- Chapter 1 prepared your mind so that you could embrace this huge opportunity with a positive attitude.
- Chapter 2 offered information about the curriculum.
- Chapter 3 detailed the examination process.
- Chapter 4 delved deeper into making yourself known in the groups where your prospective students are hanging out.
- Chapter 5 gave practical tips on how to deal with parents and manage your payments.
- Chapter 6 gave you all the advice you need to set up your website and organize your resources online.
- Chapter 7 encouraged you to let your practice grow and showed you how to implement time multipliers to help you manage the growth well.

WORDS OF ENCOURAGEMENT

I have been where you are, wondering how to make ends meet but not wanting to give up teaching to pursue a more lucrative career. Isn't it good to know that you can establish a teaching practice and make extra money while still doing the job you love?

If you experience hiccups once you get going with your practice, it doesn't mean that you're not smart, skilled, or capable. When things go wrong, it doesn't mean you must give up.

Maybe, when things aren't going the way you had hoped or anticipated, it's because you are too close to identify the problem. That's a typical human trait—we become blind to our faults and cannot see past our problems, but we are able to see those of others and offer advice quite clearly. Be careful who you go to for help, though. People who are not like-minded may encourage you to stop and tell you that this idea won't work.

It's important to have somebody, a coach or a consultant for example, who can look at your practice from the outside, see things you can't, and advise you of a way forward.

If teaching internationally appeals to you and you need guidance from an expert, I'm happy to help. Get my training at teachinternationally.online/onlineteaching.

I look forward to meeting you and helping you establish a successful tutoring practice of your own.

If you enjoyed this book, please leave a review on Amazon and recommend it to all your teacher friends.

Best wishes for a prosperous future,

Nervana Elkhadragy

JUST FOR YOU!

A Special Gift for Teachers

Are you interested in independent teaching? Included with your purchase is our FREE guide: *"The Secret to Getting Your First Student Enroll in Your Online Class Now! The Ultimate System for a Quick, Hassle free, Teaching Practice Startup."*

Visit the link below and let us know which email address to deliver it to.

https://www.teachinternationally.online/3secrets

NOTES

INTRODUCTION

1. https://en.wikipedia.org/wiki/Chipotle_Mexican_Grill

1. DISCOVER THE OPPORTUNITY

1. https://www.statista.com/statistics/1227098/number-of-pupils-in-secondary-education-worldwide/
2. https://www.epi.org/publication/the-teacher-shortage-is-real-large-and-growing-and-worse-than-we-thought-the-first-report-in-the-perfect-storm-in-the-teacher-labor-market-series/
3. https://www.drwaynedyer.com/

2. GETTING STARTED

1. https://www.rediff.com/getahead/2005/jan/31igcse.htm
2. https://en.wikipedia.org/wiki/International_General_Certificate_of_Secondary_Education
3. https://help.cambridgeinternational.org/hc/en-gb/articles/203494082-What-is-the-difference-between-IGCSE-Core-and-Extended
4. https://www.cambridgeinternational.org/about-us/what-we-do/facts-and-figures/
5. https://www.cambridgeinternational.org/programmes-and-qualifications/cambridge-upper-secondary/cambridge-igcse/subjects/
6. https://www.cambridgeinternational.org/programmes-and-qualifications/cambridge-upper-secondary/cambridge-igcse/subjects/
7. https://www.cambridgeinternational.org/Images/412121-igcse-9-1-grading-factsheet.pdf

8. https://qualifications.pearson.com/en/subjects.html
9. https://www.oxfordaqaexams.org.uk/subjects/

3. PREPARING STUDENTS FOR EXAMS

1. https://papers.gceguide.com/IGCSE/
2. https://www.igcsevideos.com/
3. https://www.cambridgeinternational.org/support-and-training-for-schools/professional-development/courses/extension-training/online-marking-workshops/
4. https://help.cambridgeinternational.org/hc/en-gb
5. https://www.cambridgeinternational.org/support-and-training-for-schools/professional-development/courses/extension-training/online-marking-workshops/
6. https://qualifications.pearson.com/en/support/training-from-pearson-uk.html
7. https://qualifications.pearson.com/en/support/training-from-pearson-uk.html
8. https://qualifications.pearson.com/content/dam/pdf/Support/Training/guide-to-booking-onto-training.pdf
9. https://www.oxfordaqaexams.org.uk/support/events

5. COMMUNICATING WITH PARENTS AND ACCEPTING PAYMENTS

1. https://www.paypal.com/be/smarthelp/article/what-is-paypal-and-how-does-it-work-faq1655
2. https://www.freshbooks.com/hub/payments/what-is-stripe

6. WHEN WOULD YOU NEED A WEBSITE?

1. https://videofruit.com/blog/kajabi-vs-teachable-vs-thinkific/
2. https://ddiy.co/thinkific-review/

7. SECRETS TO SCALING YOUR PRACTICE

1. https://www.forbes.com/sites/kimberly-whitler/2014/07/17/why-word-of-mouth-marketing-is-the-most-important-social-media/?sh=48d31e8e54a8

REFERENCES

A guide to A*–G and 9–1 grades. (2017, October). Cambridge Assessment International Education. https://www.cambridgeinternational.org/Images/412121-igcse-9-1-grading-factsheet.pdf

Booking onto a training event: A step by step guide. (2021, July). Pearson Education. https://qualifications.pearson.com/content/dam/pdf/Support/Training/guide-to-booking-onto-training.pdf

Cambridge IGCSE subjects. (n.d.). Cambridge Assessment International Education. https://www.cambridgeinternational.org/programmes-and-qualifications/cambridge-upper-secondary/cambridge-igcse/subjects/

Chipotle Mexican Grill. (2021, November 17). Wikipedia. https://en.wikipedia.org/ wiki/Chipotle_Mexican_Grill

Cudd, G. (2021, November 3). *My honest review of Thinkific.* Don't Do It Yourself. https://ddiy.co/ thinkific-review/

Facts and figures about Cambridge International. (n.d.). Cambridge Assessment International Education. https://www.cambridgeinternational.org/about-us/ what-we-do/facts-and-figures/

Garcia, E. & Weiss, E. (2019, March 26). *The teacher shortage is real, large and growing, and worse than we thought.* Economic Policy institute. https://www.epi. org/publication/the-teacher-shortage-is-real-large-and-growing-and-worse-than-we-thought-the-first-report-in-the-perfect-storm-in-the-teacher-labor-market-series/

Harris, B. (2021, January 14). *Kajabi vs Thinkific vs Teachable: A balanced comparison (with recommendations).* Growth Tools. https://videofruit.com/blog/kajabi-vs-teachable-vs-thinkific/

International General Certificate of Secondary Education. (2021, July 12). Wikipedia. https://en.wikipedia.org/ wiki/International_General_Certificate_of_Secondary _Education

Live training. (n.d.). Pearson Education. https://qualifications.pearson.com/en/support/training-from-pearson-uk.html

Online marking workshops. (n.d.). Cambridge Assessment International Education. https://www.cambridgeinternational.org/support-and-training-for-schools/professional-development/courses/extension-training/online-marking-workshops/

Past papers of: Cambridge IGCSE. (n.d.). GCE Guide. https://papers.gceguide.com/IGCSE/

Pearson qualifications: Find a subject. (n.d.). Pearson Education. https://qualifications.pearson.com/en/subjects.html

Subjects. (n.d.). Oxford International AQA Examinations. https://www.oxfordaqaexams.org.uk/subjects/

Szmigiera, M. (2021, July 18). *Number of pupils in secondary education worldwide from 2000 to 2019.* Statista. https://www.statista.com/statistics/1227098/number-of-pupils-in-secondary-education-worldwide/

Tikmany, R. (2005, January 31). *The IGCSE education: How can it help your child?* Rediff News. https://www.rediff.com/getahead/2005/jan/31igcse.htm

Training and events. (n.d.). Oxford International AQA Examinations. https://www.oxfordaqaexams.org.uk/support/events

What can we help you with? (n.d.). Cambridge Assessment International Education. https://help.cambridgeinternational.org/hc/en-gb

What is PayPal and how does it work. (n.d.). PayPal. https://www.paypal.com/be/smarthelp/article/what-is-paypal-and-how-does-it-work-faq1655

What is Stripe and how does it work? (n.d.). Fresh Books. https://www.freshbooks.com/hub/payments/what-is-stripe

What is the difference between IGCSE Core and Extended? (n.d.). Cambridge Assessment International Education. https://help.cambridgeinternational.org/hc/en-gb/articles/203494082-What-is-the-difference-between-IGCSE-Core-and-Extended

Whitler, K. A. (2014, July 17). *Why word of mouth marketing is the most important social* media. Forbes. https://www.forbes.com/sites/kimberlywhitler/2014/07/17/why-word-of-mouth-marketing-is-the-most-important-social-media/?sh=48d31e8e54a8

Printed in Great Britain
by Amazon